As Fit as a Fish –

the English and Italians revealed

As Fit as a Fish

LAURA TOSI AND PETER HUNT

Illustrated by Jane Stevenson

Patrician Press ● Manningtree

Laura Tosi is Professor of English Literature at Venice University, specialising in early modern drama and children's literature. She has spent a lot of time in the UK and is still trying to understand the English.

Peter Hunt is retired Professor of Children's Literature from Cardiff University, and in autumn 2013 was visiting Professor in Venice where he discovered spritz and, to his surprise, was not kidnapped by the mafia.

Between them they have published around thirty academic books but *As Fit as a Fish* is a new venture!

Jane Stevenson was born in London, and brought up in Beijing, London and Bonn. She is an academic by profession and also the author of two collections of novellas and four novels. She has always drawn for pleasure, and occasionally for publication.

Published by Patrician Press 2015

For more information: www.patricianpress.com

First published as a paperback edition by Patrician Press 2015
E-book edition published by Patrician Press 2015

Text copyright © Laura Tosi and Peter Hunt 2015

Illustrations copyright © Jane Stevenson 2015

British Library Cataloguing in Publication Data. A catalogue record for this book is available from the British Library.

ISBN 978-0-9930106-4-4

Printed and bound in Peterborough by Printondemand-worldwide

www.patricianpress.com

Contents

Introduction

This is a book about the odd, the unexpected: it's about demolishing stereotypes and celebrating differences. It's about the joy of surprise.

To begin with, it's called *As Fit as a Fish* because that's the Italian equivalent of the English idiom *As Fit as a Fiddle* or *As Fit as a Flea*. Language looks at the world differently.

Of course, the Italians and the English know a lot about each other. Fifty years ago, Italy was a strange place for the English, full of Vespas and spaghetti harvests, ice-cream sellers, and families of ten eating pasta. But the easyJet generation (and easyJet is, let us not forget, the biggest internal air carrier in Italy) knows better than this – that all Italians don't look like Marcello Mastroianni and Sophia Loren, and, equally, that the English don't *all* wear bowler hats, live in thatched cottages, and eat bad food.

… But what do they *really* know? This book aims to fill the gaps.

After all, when an Englishperson goes to Italy, or an Italian goes to England, they take with them preconceptions and prejudices: for example –

Italians as seen by the English	*English as seen by the Italians*
1 Excitable and passionate	1 Uptight and eccentric
2 Unreliable	2 Like fair play
3 Ruled by the Mafia and	3 Entranced by the Royal Family
4 Dirty	4 Dirty
... what?	

And on the subject of the Mafia, in August 2014, the English perfumiers Shay and Blue found themselves in a spot of bother after introducing their *Sicilian Limes* perfume with the tag line 'can provoke vendettas'. 'Ruthlessly risky,' the text went on: 'from Sicily, home of the mafia.' The last part of this was cut after complaints from the Italian ambassador. But in a typically Italian apologetic tone, the journalist of the newspaper *Il fatto quotidiano* who reported the event, took some of the blame: 'we don't do much as a country to tell the world that we are different [from this].'

The English are still surprised – not to say outraged – that Italian visitors to England are shocked at how dirty the houses are: after all, the Italians live in the sunshine and are covered with dust and are... *foreign!*

Equally, Italians can identify the English by three almost-capital sins:

1 eating coloured pasta
2 drinking cappuccino after 12 am[1]
and 3, men wearing short socks.

---

[1] or even 10 am. Beppe Severgnini in the essential *La Bella Figura* says 'After ten o'clock in the morning, it is unethical, and possibly even unlawful, to order one.'

… while the English are bemused by the Italians

1 allowing children into restaurants in the evening
2 expecting you to help yourself to wine at dinner
and 3, kissing between (straight) men.

So, this is an eccentric, sideways view of two countries. The English struggle to understand *fare bella figura* – the totally untrivial Italian triumph of style over substance, while the Italians struggle to understand English understatement.[2]

One of the best we have seen was on a notice-board outside a church: 'Death? A Bit of a Worry, Isn't It?'

And then there is embarrassment – or the lack of it. The American writer Sarah Lyall, in her book *A Field Guide to the British*, which is about her experience of 'going native' in England, describes how when she fell downstairs at her hairdresser's, and was in agony, her 'overwhelming emotion was embarrassment. I said "Sorry" in a meek little voice. Then… "I might possibly at some point need an ambulance."' That wouldn't have happened in Italy: sympathetic help would have flowed from all sides; the victim would have expressed her pain very vocally: Italy is NOT a land of embarrassment! (Unless, of course, you mention in many quarters, one S. Berlusconi.)

So this book is about peanut spoons, wedding menus, underwear, and early modern tourists: it can hardly avoid being about politics and driving habits, but mostly it is about food, drink, rituals and real life.

And, of course, a lot of real life is the same in England and in Italy: the local papers in Venice have headlines about clam smuggling;

---

[2] Kate Fox, in *Watching the English* gives a good example: an Anglophile Italian friend 'was describing, heatedly and at some length, a ghastly meal he had had at a local restaurant - the food was inedible, the place was disgustingly filthy, the service rude beyond belief, etc., etc. "Oh," said my father, at the end of the tirade, "So, you wouldn't recommend it, then?" "YOU SEE?" cried his Italian friend. "That's it! How do you *do* that? How do you *know* to do that? How do you know *when* to do it?"'

local papers in Gloucestershire have headlines about thieves stealing copper pipes from a newly built police station. Things LOOK the same: an Italian visitor to England may have to look the wrong way when crossing the road, and English visitors to Italy might forget to pay for drinks at a café-bar because they are not required to do so immediately. But, not far beneath the surface, things are different.

This book tries to sneak beneath the surface.

Two final points before, dear readers, you launch into the book.

The first is that we don't aim to be comprehensive or impartial (although we do aim to be accurate – and all the figures quoted are genuine, although not precise to three decimal points – this is not a thesis!)[3] This book was written by a middle-aged Northern-Italian female and a middle-class Midland-English male (about as culturally opposite as you can get) and any other combination of prejudices and self-righteousness would have produced a very different book.

Secondly, this book is about the *English* and the *Italians*. There are probably great books to be written about the Scots and the Italians, and the Welsh and the Italians, and so on, or about the Sicilians and the English or the Tuscans and the Welsh – but this is not any of those.

There is a paradox here, straight away. We are told that Italy is a volatile state, and the United Kingdom a stable state: the United Kingdom has been united since 1707 (and fine-tuned in 1801 and 1922), whereas united Italy dates only from 1861. However, in Italy, Italians know what it is to be Italian: nobody is quite sure in Britain what it means to be British – as the recent attempt of the Scots to secede from the 'Union' demonstrates. As the ironic Englishman Michael Flanders observed, 'The rule is, if we have done anything good "it's another triumph for Great Britain." If we haven't, it's "England loses again."'

---

[3] We sometimes quote figures for England, and sometimes for the United Kingdom, but only when separate figures for England are not available.

11

And so, if anyone from Wales or Scotland or Northern Ireland wants to identify with the English character portrayed in this book, they are most welcome! Similarly, we are well aware that there is not one 'Italy' lurking on the peninsula, any more than there is one England – and so we apologise in advance for some heady generalisations.

For example – here's two to start off with:

– the English envy the Italians' apparently effortless elegance – all those top fashion brands – and their spontaneity – their *sprezzatura*;

– the Italians envy the English spirit of fair play and reliability – in June 2014, a Colonel in the Carabinieri, Roberto Zuliani, from Padua, who has investigated cases of bribery and fraud said: 'We have to start putting honest and competent people in the right places... We should start being less Italian and more Anglo Saxon...'

So – welcome! *Benvenuti!* to an adventure into the unlikely, a world where Latina (founded by Mussolini in 1932) is twinned with Birkenhead (dating from the 12th century, and with the oldest publicly-funded park in England), Lucca with Abingdon (distinguished as the largest town in England without a railway station), and Pesaro (with its 5th century Cathedral Basilica and its beaches) with Watford – and very little is what it might seem.

Chapter 1

The English, the Italians and the Others

> Heaven would be an English policeman, a German engineer, a French chef, an Italian lover, and everything run by the Swiss... Hell would be an English chef, a German policeman, a French engineer, a Swiss lover, and everything run by the Italians...
> – *Old English Joke*

When it comes to the unfortunate foreigners, the English have a reputation for arrogance that goes back a long way. In 1908, a critic writing about books for boys, and especially those written by the prolific Empire-builder G. A. Henty, said:

> There is no doubt that the immortal Henty and his hosts of imitators have made the British nation the most conceited people on this earth... After fourteen or fifteen years' perusal of 'piffle' written apparently for his edification, the young Englishman leaves home and country with the very firm idea in his head that he, personally, is equal to two or more Frenchmen, about four Germans, an indefinite number of Russians, and any quantity you care to mention of the remaining scum of the earth.
> – R. van Eeghen, *The Captain.*

And it's surprising that, despite Empire shrinking into Commonwealth, and global influence collapsing, these attitudes linger.

Embattled Britannia

FOG IN THE CHANNEL: EUROPE ISOLATED

– legendary English Newspaper Headline

> The English, the English, the English are best
> I wouldn't give tuppence for all of the rest!
> – *Michael Flanders and Donald Swann*

In contrast, Italians don't have a superiority complex when it comes to other European nations – they implicitly believe they are in an 'A' category along with France, England, Germany and Spain... and they are often quite surprised when they realise that the first three of these countries put Italy in the 'B' category. (Most Italians would probably classify Eastern bloc or African countries as 'B'.)

Like the English, the Italians are proud of their past and their culture – tourism is a huge industry in both countries. And both countries neglect their treasures. Recently, an archaeologist in the Italian culture ministry, Andrea Carandini said: 'We are stunned when some walls fall down. But these are ruins not systematically maintained, so the miracle is that so few of them collapse'. Also, like the English, the Italian national sport is complaining about everything from taxation to corruption, from public service to crowded buses, from the price of fruit to politicians' high wages.

Both countries are fond of self-disparagement, although possibly for different reasons. The English are confident that whatever the economic or cultural evidence, they are the best – they have a confident irony – perhaps a little jaded – bolstered by their habit of understatement. As Flanders and Swann put it:

> The English are moral, the English are good
> And clever and modest and misunderstood.

With the Italians it is not so clear. On the one hand they seem to have an inferiority complex (there was a recent cartoon in the newspaper *La Repubblica* showing a lady looking ill, with the caption: 'I feel sick... I am either pregnant or Italian'). On the other, they can spend hours disparaging their country – especially to foreigners (possibly because they know that they are so lucky to live in Italy that they *can afford* the luxury of complaining!).

The English see themselves as living on a tight little island that has defied invaders: the Italians see themselves as a (decadent?)

country whose present is not as good as its splendid past. The economic crisis has made this feeling of *frustration* more acute, if possible. While the English see themselves as a separate island, keeping 'the continent' at a distance, Italians have always been proud of being part of Europe and the European Union (Italy was one of the six founding nations of the EU, with Belgium, France, Germany, Luxembourg and the Netherlands). In the last few years the relationship Italians have established with Europe has become more ambivalent and now many believe that the budgetary *rigour* European technocrats have imposed on Italy has put even more obstacles in the path to *economic* recovery.

(But there are some Italians who refer to the rest of the country as 'il continente' – the Sardinians!)

W*GS BEGIN AT CALAIS and other International Attitudes

As Holger Ehling put it, in *Finding England* (2012) 'Let's perhaps agree that [the English] have an actively neutral position when it comes to foreigners. Many English will tell you that some of their best friends know people who know foreigners. This attitude is, of course, rooted in history. A proud nation that once ruled a quarter of the globe cannot be blamed for thinking of itself as being a cut above the rest of us.'

We don't know whether every country has a vocabulary of insulting terms for foreigners – but the English have a remarkably comprehensive one which we won't reprint here. The novelist and social critic George Orwell somewhat piously objected, in 1940, to the endemic comic boys' school stories by Frank Richards because, among other things, they made out foreigners to be funny. To which Richards replied, 'Well, foreigners *are* funny: look at that Mr Hitler.'

Italy, it would seem, doesn't have many general terms – except perhaps for *Marocchini* (Moroccans) for all Africans and *crucchi* for Germans.[4]

...and the French

Jean Cocteau said that the French are sad Italians. Or to put it another way the French are Italians in a bad mood because, as the Italians would say, they are *not* Italian. And yet the obvious sense of superiority that the French feel towards the Italians is particularly hurtful. (Italians call the French 'our cousins' – the French do not reciprocate.) The Italians believe, after all, that they have won in ALL the traditional areas of competition: cuisine (how can you take seriously a nation that uses pasta as a side dish?), wine, fashion, and football.

Then, of course, Italians are still worried about the fact that the French have given the name to the bidet but do not know how to use it (more about this indispensable piece of bathroom furniture in the chapters to come) or the fact that they carry their baguettes under their arms (the horror!).[5]

And to such a non-nationalistic country as Italy, French nationalism seems baffling.

The English have a similarly ambivalent attitude to the French. The generations that felt superior because they had 'saved' the French in two World Wars may have faded away, but the feeling that the French are more stylish, more liberated and more sexy than the English lingers. They are now regarded as amiable, if occasionally fractious, neighbours – although the fact that they build better railways and more successful cars is harder to swallow.

---

[4] *Crucco* is an Italian adaptation of the Croatian word 'cruh' which means 'bread', a word that was used by Austrian prisoners of war of Croatian origin who would ask Italians for bread.
[5] Some Italians firmly believe that this is why the French invented perfume!

... and the Spanish

Italians think that the Italians and the Spanish really like one another and are very similar – both are culturally Catholic, with a passion for living, food, partying, and family, and they both live in sunny Mediterranean climates. Some have observed that the Spanish are passionate, while the Italians are sentimental, that the Spanish are envious, and the Italians jealous. Machismo is Spanish, *mammismo* is Italian. But we could invert the terms and still in a way things would ring true. And, of course, most Italians also think that they can speak Spanish and will be understood in Spain, or that they can understand Spanish intuitively, which of course causes a lot of mutual misunderstanding (but also much fun).

The English have had a long love affair with Spain, especially since the package holiday boom of the 1960s – the first BEA [British European Airways] flight to the 'Costa Blanca' was in 1957. Today, around 25% of Spain's tourists come from Britain – and the top three holiday destinations for the English are in Spain (Malaga, Tenerife, and Alicante) – with two more in the top ten. The only Italian destinations in the top fifty are Rome (17) and Venice (29). For the majority of the package-holidaymakers, Spain is simply England with sun, but since 1995 over 750,000 English have gone to live in Spain – a figure that is rapidly being reduced by the change in the European economy. More than 90,000 English expats returned home in 2013.

... and the Germans

While England seems to visiting Italians to be obsessed with the World Wars – and the media tend to manufacture visceral dislike of the Germans, especially over football matches – the war no longer seems to be a problem for the young generation – and this is especially so in Italy. Thanks to the Erasmus exchange programme, a lot of Italian university students spend part of their school careers abroad and Germany is a favourite destination. As in England, the oldest generation still bears grudges about the Second World War – there was a very bloody aftermath after the Italians joined the Allies in

1943, and after the war many Italian immigrants in Germany and Switzerland felt they were discriminated against.

Pane e cioccolata (*Bread and Chocolate*) is a 1974 Italian comedy-drama film which chronicled the misadventures of Nino, an Italian immigrant to Switzerland, who after losing his work permit, decides to dye his hair and moustache blonde and pass himself off as a local. But the catharsis happens in a bar, while he is watching a football match (Italy vs England at Wembley, 1973): after the Italian goal, he confesses proudly that he is Italian, so he is arrested and deported. Football is still one of the areas where the competition between Italy and Germany is stronger… Italians feel that beating the Germans *at least* at football gives unique pleasure and can't be compared to beating other nations. Many famous matches against Germany which Italy won (generally during world championships) are still in the collective memory of many Italians.

Nevertheless, Italians in Germany form one of the largest Italian diasporas in the world and account for one of the main immigrant groups in Germany. Since 1961, more than 580,000 Italians have emigrated to Germany for work, mainly from Southern and North-eastern Italy. Conversely, Italy is still one of Germany's favourite holiday destinations, especially the beaches of the Adriatic and Lake Garda. Italians complain that the Germans have no dress sense – wearing men's sandals with socks is a capital crime in Italy: if you are seen doing so, someone will point out that 'you look like a German.' (Of course, the English do this a lot, too!)

New Emigrants

> **Beppe Severgnini's Universal Rule:**
>
> In every lab/university/research centre in the world you can find, at least:
> 1 computer,
> 1 green plant,
> and 1 *Italian* working there.

The English and the Italians get around.

In recent years, more than 300,000 British left the country to live abroad – 72% to take up existing jobs: favourite destinations, Australia, the USA, and Spain. This may sound a lot, but it is nothing compared to Italy's diasporas: from 1861 to 1985 29,036,000 Italians migrated to other countries, and the flow continues. According to the latest OECD survey [Organisation for Economic Co-operation and Development] in the UK there is an almost perfect balance between the number of professionals who come to England and professionals who leave. But in Italy every unskilled immigrant labourer is counterbalanced by TWO professionals who leave: and one of the most popular destinations for the professional migrant – with an increase of 71% between 2013 and 2014 – is England.

The headmaster of Eton is Italian (from Padua). At the other cultural extreme, English bookmakers decided to support Andrea Faustini, the 20-year-old 'little Italian teddy bear' for probable winner of the 2014 UK *X Factor*. With poor English and hardly gifted with a physique du rôle, he has been described as 'The Tear Inducing Italian Sensation': the talent scout and TV celebrity Simon Cowell, after one of his performances, couldn't help shouting: 'Italy's loss, Britain's gain!' Astonishingly, Italian bookmakers decided to support the only foreign contestant in the 2014 Italian *X-Factor*, the *British* Emma Norton!

Italy is becoming a place for old people: it is third in the world age-of-population league table, with a median age of 45.6 (England is 26th, with a median age of 41.5). Power still appears to belong to the older generation, and so young Italian graduates emigrate. The Italian deputy minister for Foreign Affairs has declared that the emigration figures should not worry anyone, as this new wave of emigration is not an escape from poverty and hunger, as it was for previous generations, but a choice. But even if it *is* a choice (people who leave tell a different story) one wonders why this country is letting go of so many graduates. The reasons seem to be – lack of opportunities, low salaries, a system that is not *fair* and which does not always rewards the best, especially if the best is represented by *young* people![6]

SO:

Our idea of the Italian family (father, mother and 5 small children sitting at a table eating a mountain of spaghetti) is now completely inaccurate: the combination of one of the lowest birth rates in Europe, 43.7 % youth unemployment rate (July 2014), and the economic crisis, have created families of adults: 61% of young people from 18 to 34 years (almost 7 million people) live with at least one parent.

New Immigrants

We are looking for the unexpected – so, what would we expect national attitudes to be when it comes to immigration? Welcoming or defensive? Left wing or right wing?

Recent figures show that 7.4%-9.4% of Italy's population are foreign nationals – the figure is around 12%-13% for Britain. Over the past 70 years or so, England received several waves of immigrants – Poles and Italians immediately after the Second World War, West Indians from the 1950s and people from the Indian sub-continent in the 1960s and 1970s. Stronger controls were instituted in 1972, just as Italy's immigration levels were rising.

They rose for the same reason as England's had 25 years earlier – a shortage of unskilled labour. For Italy, this was supplied largely from the Eastern bloc countries – and, not surprisingly 86% of immigrants live in the Northern and central parts of the country (the most economically developed areas). One of the disparaging words for

---

[6] Between 1876 and 1930, for example, five million Italians emigrated to America, the largest group of new immigrants (the old immigrants being German, Irish, British, and Scandinavians throughout the 19th century). These immigrants, mostly artisans and peasants, represented all regions of Italy, but mainly came from the *Mezzogiorno,* Southern Italy.

the first African immigrants who sold (and still sell) trinkets on the beach or counterfeit handbags in the tourist centres of historical cities is *Vu cumprà*. This apparently originates from a version of Neapolitan dialect of the standard Italian *vuoi comprare?* ('you want to buy?') – possibly the first phrase in Italian that the African street and beach traders learn.

So far, so similar, although it is only comparatively recently that Italy has begun to suffer the kinds of racial tension that have been around in England since the 1950s. For Italy, the transition between a sending country to a receiving country (and now possibly again a sending country), with a society aging rapidly, hasn't been an easy one. Italy's improved education levels left many jobs open in the lower end of the market, both in the manufacturing sector and in the service sector.

Until the 1980s, Italy perceived itself as an ethnically homogeneous country.

OPRAH AND THE SHOP ASSISTANT

In one celebrated case in 2013, the American billionaire Oprah Winfrey accused an Italian shop assistant (in Zurich) of racial prejudice because she offered to show her a cheaper handbag than the €28,400 one that Oprah was looking at. The shop assistant's response might stand for the average Italian. 'I am Italian,' she said in an interview with a Swiss magazine. 'Why should I discriminate against anybody because of their origin?'

There were a lot of headlines around this time about racist attacks by the supporters of the xenophobic Lega Nord (Northern League) on Congolese-born Cécile Kyenge, Italy's first-ever black cabinet minister (she was Minister for Integration). (When she had bananas thrown at her, she responded by deploring the 'waste of food'.) Yet despite some commentators suggesting that Italy was facing an upsurge of racism not seen since the days of Mussolini, this seems to have been contradicted by the case of the immigrants crossing the Mediterranean to enter Europe (via Italy). The parallel case of immigrants crossing the English Channel to enter England equally demonstrates some curiously differing attitudes.

After a series of shipwrecks off Sicily's coast which killed hundreds of 'boat people', Italy changed its policy of blocking immigrants at sea, returning many to Libya, their main point of departure, and ran a search-and-rescue effort called *Operazione Mare Nostrum*, which rescued an estimated 150,000 refugees between October 2013 and October 2014.

After a year the Italian government talked of terminating the operation on the grounds that it was financially unsustainable (it cost €12,000,000 a month); at the same time, the British government withdrew its support for a replacement operation. The reason, that such operations were a 'pull factor' and encouraged crossings was exactly the same as that given by the leaders of the Lega Nord party in Italy, who had declared that the hands of Italy's prime minister, Matteo Renzi, and his interior minister, Angelino Alfano, were 'stained with blood'. It was not by chance that the first journey that Pope Francis took was to Lampedusa, the island off the coast of Sicily where 360 people had drowned in October 2013. 'Who has wept for the deaths of these brothers and sisters? For the young mothers carrying their babies? For these men who wanted something to support their families with?' he asked. Immigrants were given medical treatment, food and temporary shelter, and Italian laws were changed to decriminalize migrants.

The knock-on effect of the increase in the number of immigrants into Italy and thence to the rest of Europe said to be caused by the operation has been the 7,500 of people camped in Calais, trying to reach England. The English border has officially been moved to France together with €15,000,000 to try to contain the influx. Tension with the French government has risen, and even fairly moderate politicians have been led to immoderate comments about English towns being 'swamped', and the United Kingdom Independence Party has gained ground.

In Italy, the Lega Nord was at the peak of its success when allied to Berlusconi's party. At one point Giancarlo Gentilini, the infamous Mayor of Treviso from 1994 to 2003, and deputy mayor until 2013, had all the benches around the railway station removed because they were used by immigrants. Not content with that, Gentilini went further and suggested hunting the immigrants: 'we should dress them up as rabbits and go bang, bang, bang with a rifle.' Berlusconi's fall from political favour damaged the League – Gentilini tried to run again for mayor of Treviso but was defeated in 2014 by a left-wing candidate, whose view on immigration is radically different from his.

And finally

'SBAGLIA PORTA: ATTORE UBRIACO IN CASA' –

'The Wrong Door: Drunken Actor in the House.'
La Tribuna

Not long ago, after a party at the Castello di Roncade in the small town of Roncade, near Treviso, an English actor, Elliot Travers, rather the worse for wear took a taxi to his bed-and-breakfast hotel.

As he couldn't remember the name of his b+b, he got the taxi-driver to drop him somewhere in the general vicinity. At that moment, the owner of the house *next door* to the b+b (a man *not* named in the newspaper report – something that couldn't happen in England) was taking his dog for a walk, leaving his front door open by mistake. The illuminated Mr Travers found the open door, assumed that he had found his b+b, and went into the wrong house, where he used the bathroom and went to sleep on the sofa.

About two hours later, the lady of the house (equally un-named) was having breakfast, when the actor got up to have a shower, using the lady's son's bathrobe. The lady saw him walking past the kitchen, and thinking it was her son, addressed him in Italian. She heard a muffled reply in English. So she went and woke up her son and asked him whether he had a friend staying. He said no.

So they panicked, returned to the kitchen, locked themselves in, called the husband, opened the window and started shouting for help. Someone called the Carabinieri, who arrived at the same time as the husband and found the actor fast asleep in the son's bathrobe on the sofa. As he was still in a stupor, the Carabinieri took him to hospital, where he eventually revived.

Now, here is the point of the story.

The householders had, naturally, been very upset and alarmed, but when they found out that the intruder was English, *they decided not to press charges.* Why?

Well, he was *English* – and the English are perceived as harmless eccentrics, and a nation of heavy drinkers, and much more amusing than threatening. The family would definitely have pressed charges had he been of almost any other nationality – possibly with the *only* exception of the Spanish. But, being a mere *Inglese* he was allowed to get away with it!

And if that had happened in England – which nationalities would the English have forgiven? The answer might be – perhaps the Dutch or the Scandinavians, but only because the English feel that they are basically good chaps who might have gone astray. As for the rest, despite what Frank Richards thought, foreigners behaving badly are not really funny: the English might have let him off as a matter of good manners, but not as a matter of good will.

And after that simple contrast about how the people of Italy and the people of England would react, let us immediately confuse things by asking – which Italy and which England, North or South?

Chapter 2

North and South

Or, Which England? Which Italy?

> 'Garibaldi, perché?'
> (Garibaldi, why (did you do it)?)
> *Northern football supporters' banner used to insult Southern supporters.*
>
>   *
>
> 'South country people are often frightened by what our Darkshire men and women only call living and struggling.' – Mrs Gaskell, *North and South* (1855)

When the English go to Italy, they think, as Kenneth Grahame did in *The Wind in the Willows,* of the warm South – of sun and wine and beaches (except when they're thinking of churches and paintings and Venice – although there are sun and wine and beaches in Venice!) To the English, all of Italy is South: the headline picture on the official Italian tourist website (at the time of writing) is of beach umbrellas in Rimini (actually in the Northern half of Italy), and the three pictures in the 'Discover Italy' section are of Molise, Calabria, and Apulia (all South or far South)!

But just as there is more to England than London and the South, one of the things that England and Italy share is the South/North divide, a happy hunting ground for the kinds of stereotypes that we are setting out to debunk. [7]

---

[7] Of course, for this chapter to be totally unbiased at least four people should have written it: an Italian from the North, an Italian from the South, an

As Harry Mount points out in *How England Made the English* (2012), the geography of England and Italy both lend themselves to North-South splits – and the more temperate the weather, the more superior the region thinks itself. In England, the North's self image is tough and egalitarian, poor but honest; the South (and that includes London) is (according to the North) soft and snobbish, rich and unscrupulous. Southerners think the North is dark, cold, and uncivilised. In Italy, the North is efficient and soul-less; it has Milan and money – and the best hospitals (some are also research centres, collaborating with foreign universities) – so if you must be ill in Italy make sure you are ill in Lombardia, Veneto or Emilia. (Italians from the South migrate to the North to have big operations.) The South is, according to the stereotype, sunshine and the Mafia – poverty and anarchy. Anywhere South of Rome is, Northerners will tell you, ungovernable. Driving in Turin may be terrifying for the English – but compared with what happens in Naples (where we have seen tourists standing mesmerised on the pavements, wondering how drivers survive) it is a model of decorum. And no civilised person, Italian Southerners will tell you, eats pizza North of Rome.

As Peter Davidson said of Italy, in *The Idea of North* (2005)

> In no other country is 'north' a more unstable descriptor, shifting and flickering, defined and redefined minutely, almost kilometre by kilometre, the length of the peninsula. In Lucca in Tuscany they refer to the northern suburbs as 'Germany', the southern suburbs as 'Africa'.

Tourists coming to England don't seem to buy the idea that the North of England is dour and damp. London, as we might expect, captures 54% of the total spending by foreign visitors, but the most successful tourist areas are scattered across the country. York attracts marginally more visitors than Bath, the Lake District is clogged with 15.5 million tourists each year, and Blackpool – although it is hard to

---

Englishperson from the North and an Englishperson from the South. Laura is from the North, and so is naturally fair-minded and impartial, while Peter was born and raised in almost the exact centre of England – Rugby – and so regards anyone born North or South of there with equal disdain.

find evidence for the often quoted claim that it has more holiday beds than Portugal – hosts 10 million visitors a year (Italian visitors are seventh on the visitors' table).

In Italy, perhaps surprisingly, given the urge towards the sun, only 20% of foreign visitors go to the South – compared with 30% who go to Venice alone (60,000 *per day!*). Even the Italians aren't too keen: only 24% of Italians who go on holiday in their country go to the South. Why? Bad infrastructure, worse roads, slower trains, corruption – or more stereotypes? Most places are not quite what we expect.

ENGLISH DRIVER STOPS AT RED TRAFFIC LIGHT IN SALERNO

'I don't know what came over me,' said Harry Jones, from the wreckage. 'It must have been a reflex.' A city spokesman pointed out that Mr Jones, is of course, fortunate to be in Salerno, where they have the world's oldest medical school, the *Scuola Medica Salernitana*. It is not clear whether its foundation in the 9th Century was in response to traffic conditions of the time.

Before We Go Any Further...

You may have noticed that we have not tried to define where the North and South start. Both England and Italy have 'midlands' (centro) and could just as well be divided east-west over the spines of the Pennines and the Apennines – Norfolk could be contrasted with Shropshire, or Veneto with Piedmont; Italy's 57 provinces and England's counties (83 administrative, 48 ceremonial) – the numbers of both change with bewildering regularity – are all (although decreasingly) proud of their individual characters. However, the homogenisation of foods and high-streets is far more advanced in England than in Italy (apart from the Very Rich Streets where Gucci and Armani and Versace rub shoulders), and the Geordies of North-east England may feel more at home in Kent, than the Ladino speakers on the Austrian Border do with the Siculo-dialect speakers of Sicily.

Since April 2014, Cornwall has been awarded special cultural status, and so there might well be Cornish/English road signs one day. There are areas in the Dolomites, in the far North of Italy, where shoppers operate in three languages: we came across this sign (among many like it) in a Spar supermarket – Ladin[8] first, then Italian, then German:

> DÖT ĆI OS SE DEJIORËIS Y TRÖP LAPRÒ!
> QUELLO CHE VUOI TU E UN PO' DI PIÙ!
> ALLES WAS SIE SICH WÜBSCHEN UND NOCH
> MEHR!
> (ALL YOU WANT AND MORE!)

Incidentally, the name 'Dolomites' seems to have been coined (in passing) by an English publisher in 1837 in *Murray's Handbook of Southern Germany*. However, they were popularised as a tourist destination by two Englishmen: George Cheetham Churchill was a botanist, and Josiah Gilbert was a watercolour painter, who after visiting this part of the Alps with their wives, every year for four years, published a book – *The Dolomite Mountains* (London: Longman, 1864). (Deodat de Dolomieu, the son of a French marquis and geologist had passed through those mountains at the time of the French revolution and had noticed that those mountains were made of a very peculiar rock, which was later named after him.) Churchill and Gilbert wrote

> During eight weeks, and over a space of more than 200 miles, we did not meet a solitary member of that restless fraternity

---

[8] Ladin is a Romance language spoken by about 20,000 people on the Italian-Austrian border.

[the tourists] – English or foreign – and in many places were the first English people that had been seen.

That was 1861 and even by 1869 there were only 236 visitors registered in Cortina.

Soft South, Tough North

Both countries share this idea …but for different reasons.

Let us begin with two examples of the misunderstandings and paradoxes of North-Southing.

ITALIAN EATS MUSHY PEAS. REVIVED IN HOSPITAL

'I only did it for a bet,' said Gino Caponi (17), an exchange student, 'and I had drunk half a can of Newcastle Brown. I had no idea that it was actually food.' The stomach pumping at Wigan hospital was successful, and after a course of pasta injections, Signor Caponi was allowed back on the tour bus.

Travelling North in England on the west coast main line, one comes to Wigan in Lancashire – to Southerners, possibly the epitome of the funny-sounding North. Birthplace of George Formby, the hugely successful comedian of the 1930s and 1940s who made a living from being a quaint Northerner, with his little ukulele. Wigan was once a grim mill-and-mining town and George Orwell, a very upper-class Southerner increased its fame with his searing political documentary *The Road to Wigan Pier* (1937). However, anyone who follows the huge brown signs 'To Wigan Pier' on the nearby motorways may be bemused to find that it consists of two one-metre lengths of railway track on the side of a canal. Across the road from Wigan Wallgate Station (they have two) which was built by the very Northern Lancashire and Yorkshire railway, you can buy the Northern delicacy (and staple) pie and mushy peas and gravy. Nothing could be more stereotypically 'Northern'. And yet, a few yards up the hill is the picturesque Parish Church of All Saints and its churchyard, and a town centre that might be in Cambridgeshire or Suffolk. (Or, to put it another way, Bury St. Edmunds would not feel out of place in Lancashire.) Not what the prejudiced might expect.

Or, travel South in Italy to Naples.

Naples has had a bad press over the years – Northerners shake their heads when you say you are going there (much as Rotterdammers do when you say you're going to Amsterdam). But, of course, it has magnificent views, and the centre, with its markets is (contrary to expectations) rather like Bombay but without any smells. What is striking is the superstition. Walk into one of the churches off the Spaccanapoli and you are struck by the strong cult of the saints: Saint Patricia of Naples, patron saint of difficult problems, is remarkable not only for her broad portfolio but for the 'fact' that the dried sample of her blood in the Church liquefies on her feast day (25th August) *and also on every Tuesday morning*. Other local saints, such as San Luigi or San Filippo Neri, it seems, only achieve this feat annually: one 17th-century traveller called the area 'urbs sanguinum.' It does not take long to realise that this is no mere metaphor; the relics of saints across most of the South are venerated for such literal manifestations. Even among the most educated Southerners, a belief in the evil eye – the unlucky effect of some people – and the use of lucky charms persists.

Of course, some of the superstition has a pragmatic element. In July 2014 Bishop Francesco Milito of Oppido Mamertina-Palmi in Calabria banned religious processions after the men carrying a statue of the Virgin Mary, and hundreds of followers, paused during a procession in Tresilico, and bowed to the house of a Mafia boss. As the Bishop said, they were 'clearly far from even a minimum spirit of pure, correct and authentic faith.'

Back to the Stereotypes

Many of the old dividing characteristics between North and South remain in the UK, often complicated by 'class' issues. In 2013, Surrey sent more students to Oxford and Cambridge than Wales and the North-east combined; MPs from the North (especially women) have been mocked in the House of Commons for their accents. Things are even more extreme in Italy.

There (depending on which lens you look through), the North is efficient and dull, the South inefficient but fun. In Milan, where business meetings and conferences run on time, a business lunch takes twenty minutes; in Naples, a business lunch is a four-course affair, and conferences start when everybody is there. Northerners are pale and cold and sad; they live inside because it is freezing and foggy; Southerners are tanned, live in the sun, and are always happy and in love. In possibly one of the funniest Italian films ever, *Totò, Peppino e la Malafemmina* (1956) (*Totò, Peppino and the Bad Woman*), a couple of Neapolitan brothers decide to go to the North to persuade a nephew (who has abandoned his medical studies to pursue a dancer in Milan) to come back home with them. They arrive in late spring in Milan dressed in fur coats and hats and they ask a Milanese policeman for directions *in French*.

But some prejudices retain a factual basis. In Italy, Northerners are less devoted to the family unit, while the South is more traditional and relies on 'family values'. The sociologist Edward Banfield, author of the classic *The Moral Basis of a Backward Society* (1958), studied Southern Italian communities, and noticed the inability of the villagers to act together for their common good or, indeed, for any end transcending the immediate, material interest of the nuclear family. He maintains that the South concentrates on the family as the unit of social organisation, which supersedes the State. This would apply very well to the structure of criminal organisations like the Mafia: being faithful to the family and the clan is more important than being faithful to the State.

The North, it is said, lives in the future, the South is stuck in the past. Curiously, in many regions of the South the old-fashioned *Voi* (first person plural, as the French *Vous*) instead of *Lei* (third

32

person singular, as the German *Sie*) is used when talking formally. This use of *Voi* is so completely non-existent in the North that if addressed in this way, a Northerner is quite likely to look around to see whether the Southerner is addressing someone else as well.

Equally, in both countries, some prejudices don't stand up to factual scrutiny. Manchester has a reputation for being wet (806 mm of rain per year) – but has almost exactly the same amount of rain as Brighton (801 mm): come to that, it has much less than Naples (1006 mm) – and London (601 mm) is much dryer than Rome (834 mm).[9]

Northern readers of *La Repubblica* recently named the biggest difference between North and South: Northerners *obey the law*. And yet, if we look at data provided by Giovanni Floris (*Separati in patria*, 2009), Bologna has the most armed robberies, Modena has the most burglaries, and Genova has the most pickpockets. On the other hand, the South has a well-established counter-culture: one worker in five is illegal and tax evasion is more widespread. At the same time, the Mafia now seems to have changed its methods and has moved to the North, where legal businesses are used for laundering money. The North is richer, and the Mafia follows the money. As the Italian proverb says, 'Tutto il mondo è paese' ('all the world is a village'): in 2014 the mayor of Venice had to resign for taking bribes and a number of local administrators from Milan involved in the 2015 International Exposition have been accused of the same crime.

Fact and Fiction

Giovanni Floris's *Separati in patria* is about two parallel lives, those of two children: Mr Cacace's son, born somewhere in the South, and Mr Brambilla's, born in the North. Little Cacace couldn't get into nursery school, little Brambilla could: there are 617 public nursery schools in Lombardy (27,000 places), Molise has six (219 places); 59% of these schools are in the North, 14% in the South. Mrs

---

[9] For some curious reason, the Italian half of the writing team refuses to believe these easily-verifiable-on-the-net statistics, which may say something about the Italian character, or maybe just says something about the Italian half of the writing team.

Brambilla kept her job, while Mrs Cacace had to leave work to take care of her sick parents (Mrs Brambilla's parents were also sick but the council provided care for them). Little Cacace spent his first years mainly at home with his mother and grandparents. They didn't have many visitors, but his mother talked to him all the time, and worried when he started going out with friends, as they all spoke dialect. Little Brambilla grew up in a more stimulating environment: his mother's colleagues came often to visit and he was admitted to the adult table: his linguistic abilities were remarkable for his age. At school Cacace was heroic – most of his schoolmates left school at 14, but he struggled on. Both boys eventually graduated, but Cacace was hampered by the lack of public libraries (more than 50% are in the North, and only 28.7% in the South. The highest percentage of families who don't own a single book in the house is in the South (19.2%).) Brambilla got a job easily – Cacace spent three years before he found a steady job, and for that he had to move North, where he met Brambilla at last. They arrived at the same place but the journey had been much harder for the man from the South.

Their very different lives are based on statistics on the relationship between the sexes, education and the job market across Italy. The male is the only breadwinner in 28% of Southern families (19% in the North); in the South 28% of husbands and wives share the housework (43% in the North). Children and teenagers help in the house only if they come from the North. The average annual income (at the time of writing) across Italy is €18,324, but in the South it is €14,626 (in Lombardy it is €20,172, in Calabria it is less than €11,000). At the extremes, the village of Ayas, near Aosta, in the far North-west, near the Mont Blanc tunnel is the richest in Italy, with an average annual income of €66,000. Platì, in Calabria at the very toe of Italy, and notorious for a time as the centre for the 'Ndrangheta crime organisation is the poorest, with an annual income of €4000.

A rough interpretation of the above figures? The North is rich, the South is poor, the North is productive, the South isn't. The real gap between North and South is a gap of opportunities. Being born in the South or the North makes a difference, and it is worse to be born South of Rome. *One nationality, two nations.*

Rather similar figures could be given for England, of course. In 2011, the *British Medical Journal* estimated that Northerners are 20% more likely to die before the age of 75 than Southerners; the North-East has the lowest median wage (£24,500) and the South-east the highest (£35,000); there are twice as many millionaire households in the South-east than in the North-east.

But, as always, these figures need some qualification. Italy's economy is not skewed, as England's is, by having the vast economic vacuum-cleaner of London, which sucks up huge amounts of infrastructure spending: recently it was estimated that 80% of cranes at work in England were working in London. Italy has, in effect, two capitals – Milan for finance and business, Rome for government and the headquarters or main offices of everything, from embassies to cultural institutions.

And there are exceptions to both North-South generalisations. Some of the richest communities in England – Alderley Edge, Ilkley, Harrogate – are in the North, and some of the poorest – Tower Hamlets and Hackney – in the South. In Italy, one of the most well-off and well-organized, as well as beautiful regions is Puglia – and one of the best places to visit there is Lecce. If it wasn't for the sun, the delicious food, the baroque architecture, and the dark-eyed local beauties, you would think you were in Switzerland. (Although as from the summer of 2014 you might have problems finding a hotel, after the success of the party film *Walking on Sunshine* which was filmed in Lecce.)

Filmography

Now that television detectives detect all over England – *DCI Banks* is set in Yorkshire, the 100 episodes of *Midsomer Murders* were set in an all-purpose Southern county (and deliberately excluded ethic minorities on the grounds that – according to the producer – 'it wouldn't be the English village with them'), and *Lewis* features a Geordie detective in Oxford, nowhere is unfamiliar. (The fictitious Denton in *A Touch of Frost* was located somewhere in Oxfordshire and shot in Yorkshire.) Similarly, the distinctive genres of Northern or Southern films has died out. Gone are the days when gritty Northern films such as *Saturday Night and Sunday Morning* (1960) contrasted with the Southern idyll of *Happy is the Bride* (1958) ('If you want to impress your future father-in-law, I'd let him bowl you out, old chap'), or the slick swinging London of *Nothing But the Best* (1964) (*Il Cadavere in Cantina* (*The Corpse in the Cellar*) in Italian!) contrasted with the grim grey Newcastle of *Get Carter* (1971) ('I only came back to this crap hole to find out who murdered my brother').

In Italy, though, making fun of North and South stereotypes continues: in *Benvenuti al Sud* (*Welcome to the South*) (2010) a Northern director of a post office is transferred to the South as a punishment. After the initial shock he really starts to enjoy life – so much so that he goes back home to Milan less frequently and discourages his wife from coming to see him on the grounds of the criminality, the dirt, and the Mafia. So when she does decide to take the plunge and visit him he needs a plan: with the post office employees, who have become his friends, he builds what resembles a film set, in which all the people from the village play the part of a Mafia boss, or a kidnapper, or a pickpocket. Everyone shouts and behaves like lunatics and the wife almost believes that her husband has ended up in hell. In the follow-up, *Benvenuti al Nord* (2012) an employee from the same post office is sent to the North and is lost in the fog, but after the initial shock, starts to appreciate the ways of the North.

It all started with Garibaldi

The fault-line between North and South in England runs, naturally, through the Midlands, along the old Roman Watling Street (street, of course from the Latin *via strata*). From the ninth century the Danes occupied the lands to the North, the Anglo-Saxons to the South. Place names remain, accents and vowels linger – but that was all a very long time ago. In Italy the fault-lines are much more recent: it was only in the First World War, when Italians from different regions fought in the trenches, that the Fratelli d'Italia (the Brothers of Italy, as in the first line of the national anthem), despite their different languages and dialects, discovered that they belonged to a nation.

When Garibaldi met Mazzini in the first half of the 19th century and they started dreaming of a united Italy, the North was divided between the Kingdom of Sardinia and Piedmont (the North-west) and the Kingdom of the Augsburgs (the North-east). The centre belonged to the Church (except for Tuscany, under Augsburg control), and the South to the house of Bourbon – the two Sicilies. In the North they learned to make spritz, and developed bureaucracy and punctuality; in the South they had the Enlightenment, the first chair of Political Economy (established in 1755 at the University of Naples) and the first railway line (1839).

By the end of Garibaldi's revolution the Bourbons were defeated, and the South was rich. Naples was one of the most intellectually advanced cities of Europe, with 113 printing presses, efficient sewers, drinkable water in all houses, illuminated streets, and the first observatory in Italy. The first Italian transatlantic ship, called *Sicilia*, was built in Naples and sailed between Palermo and New York. But after the unification, the civil war in the South between the State and the Southern brigands, negated these advantages. As Giovanni Floris has observed, 'The South paid the price for a united Italy.' Now, the Italian constitution guarantees the right to a form of double allegiance: you can be Sardinian or Tuscan, but Italy will be your home. One country, but many differences.

And, Finally, some Insults

There is a long tradition of insults between the North and the South, and Italians are particularly good at it. The Northerners call the Southerners *terroni* (peasants) and the Southerners call the Northerners, *polentoni* (polenta eaters). The art of insult reaches its peak on the football terraces. For example, when Naples played in Turin a few seasons ago, one of the banners said 'Benvenuti in Italia' ('Welcome to Italy'). The eighties were dominated by the rivalry between Naples and Verona – when the Veronese supporters got to Naples they carried a banner saying 'Vesuvius, do your job', and when the Neapolitans went to Verona their banner read 'Juliet is a whore'. Not sure that England can compete with that, North or South!

Insults are so culturally overloaded that, like jokes, they are difficult to translate. In the next chapter we look at attitudes to language-learning in the two cultures over the centuries.

Chapter 3

Learning English, Learning Italian

BILINGUAL ENGLISHMAN ARRESTED AT ROME AIRPORT

Simon Jones (35) was arrested after ordering a coffee at
Rome airport *in perfect Italian*. 'We assumed that he must be
a spy,' said a police spokesperson.

Learning English is one of the Italians' obsessions – to the
point that they always feel they have to apologise for not being able to
speak it. Of course, the English occasionally apologise for not being
able to speak another language, but they rarely mean it. A young
student friend of ours met an Italian girl on the Dover-Calais ferry,
and apologised for not being able to speak Italian (mostly in order to
ingratiate himself, of course!) She replied, seriously, 'Who wants to
speak Italian?'

Five hundred years ago, the dialogue would have been very
different. One of the conversations in John Florio's Italian primer,
First Fruits (1597) runs

> 'What thinke you of this Englishe tongue, tel me, I pray you?'
> 'It is a language that wyl do you good in England, but passe
> Douer, it is worth nothing.'

And the monoglot Englishman was more to be pitied than
censured – as Florio said –

> What a shame it is, that you shall see an Englishman come in
> company of strangers, who can neither speak, nor understand
> with them, but stands as one mute, & so is mocked of them,

and despised of all, and none will make account of him? What a shame is that?... What a loss to him? And what heart's grief to think thereon?

Not today.

Hordes of Italian teenagers invade the South of England every summer to learn or perfect their English. London is one of Italians' favourite destinations, and they can generally be recognised by the fact that they are holding the green *Guida del Touring* – the equivalent of the *Baedeker* of the Grand Tour! – and by the backpacks full of raincoats and sweaters – they were told that English weather is changeable. In the language schools south of London, some stay in colleges and tend to hang around with other Italians and speak Italian; some stay with English families and speak English (and can't wait to complain to other Italians – in Italian). Both categories have to struggle with the strange foreign food, shockingly different standards of cleanliness – and their best English is usually practised on the German or Spanish girl or boy with whom they invariably fall in love.

Both the English and the Italians think that their counterparts' attitude to teaching in general is eccentric.

Italians now start studying English at the age of six, and continue throughout their education – in middle school (11-14) they add another compulsory language to English. The main foreign language used to be French – a good way to find out a person's age is to ask whether they did French or English at school. If they did only French, chances are that they are over 50!

In England, enthusiasm for learning languages is more theoretical than real – and the overall picture is disastrous: as one recent headline said – 'Is Britain turning into a nation of monoglots?' (Or, as we say in English, the *lingua franca* of the world, *'Plus ça change, c'est plus la même chose'.*)

In 2004, it was no longer compulsory to study a foreign language in secondary schools in England. As a result, the number of universities offering degrees in modern languages has collapsed from 105 in 2000 to 62 in 2013 – and many as 40% of university language departments are likely to close in the next ten years.[10] The attempt to reverse this trend, by teaching languages in primary schools is hampered by the fact that around 10% of schools have no teachers with *any* knowledge of a foreign language, so the idea that from 2014 students aged seven to 11 will be required to reach 'a high standard of written and spoken communication' in *one of seven languages* – French, German, Mandarin, Spanish, Latin and Greek ... and Italian – sounds a trifle ambitious.

DUTCH PHILOSOPHER TURNS IN HIS GRAVE

Basel Minster in Switzerland was disturbed last night by rumblings from the tomb of Desiderius Erasmus Roterodamus, the famous humanist after whom the ERASMUS student-exchange programme was named. Local scholars think that the soul of Erasmus, who hated English ale and English weather when he studied in Cambridge, was protesting about English students who don't speak other languages.

So, while English diplomats and businessmen are tearing their hair over what looks like an attitude to language learning consisting of a mixture of xenophobia, laziness and arrogance, young Italian students are making the most of their opportunities to learn English.

The ERASMUS programme, which allows students to move between universities in 33 countries, is very popular in Italy: there are always more candidates than placements and new exchange programmes are set up every year. For Italians, England is the

---

[10] This is SO depressing to the English half of the authors of this book that we are going to hide even more depressing statistics down here: from 2004 to 2010, the proportion of students taking language GCSEs (at age 15) fell to just over 40%. The number of A-level candidates (at the end of high school) for French and German fell by 50%. (Italian hardly comes into the equation).

preferred destination (Italy is the third most popular destination for English students, after France and Spain) and it has become normal for Italian students to do their degree in more than one country/university, taking classes and exams in a foreign language. But things are (as we might expect by now) different the other way around – the UK does not use all the allocated European funding for the Erasmus exchange programme and often, when English students come to Italy, they take their courses in English (thereby cleverly defeating the object of the exercise).

But that doesn't mean that the English are unadventurous. In the UK, the GAP year – between school and university – is still *the* thing. It doesn't exist in Italy, but the English teenager, equipped with *no* language skills, but the sublime knowledge that the rest of the human race is busily learning English, heads off around the world. In 2012 an estimated 2.5 million students were planning a GAP year, and British parents spend as much as £995 million a year in helping to fund their children's travels! And then the students come back to England to work (with luck).

But where does the Italian Erasmus generation go, after their graduation? Abroad of course! It has been estimated that 20,000 Italian graduates go and work abroad every year. It is as if every year a village of expertise and competence migrates.

But it wasn't always like that. Or was it?

Five hundred years ago, it was the other way around: Italy was the place to be, and Italian was the language to learn, although then, as now, Italy was a tricky place.

PRINCESS'S TUTOR ATTACKS FOREIGN TRAVEL

'The Italianate Englishman is a devil incarnate,' claims
Roger Ascham in his new book *The Schoolmaster*. 'Italy is
the place to pick up vices and loose morals: there is no room
for this kind of behaviour in the modern English world of
1570.'

To judge from Shakespeare's comedies, Italy was seen as the
most advanced civilization of the time in the fields of art, music,
literature, and, perhaps more questionably, political science, fencing –
and banking. But equally, to judge from the many revenge tragedies
(such as *The Duchess of Malfi*) set in Italian palaces inhabited by
murderous dukes and cardinals, it was also seen as the cradle of
political instability, religious fanaticism, sexual corruption – and, of
course, Machiavellian machinations. (So not much has changed there
either!)

Horatio Pallavicino, who after a lifetime of European
diplomacy settled in England, expanded on Ascham's idea: if Italy
turns Englishmen into devils, 'an Italian Anglified, Becomes a Saint
Angelified'.

But, generally, the Italians didn't learn English: the English, on
the other hand, made great efforts to learn Italian. The first grammar
of Italian for English students was *Principal Rules of Italian
Grammar*, published in 1548 by a remarkable Welshman, William
Thomas. In the preface to the *Principal Rules* he writes that Italian is
the third language, after Latin and Greek, in an ideal chart of the best
languages – but, unlike Greek and Latin, Italian is 'easily obtained in a
short space.' It has, however, the same richness as the classical
languages: 'you shall almost find no part of the sciences, no part of
any worthy history, no part of eloquence, not any part of any poesie,
that you have not in the Italian tongue.'[11]

---

[11] Thomas was a very interesting character: he also wrote what was possibly
the first English book about Italy, *The History of Italy* (1549). His career, was

From the 1540s, first-generation Italian immigrants tutored the English aristocracy privately; by the 1570s, private language schools teaching *Italian* (and French) were booming in London and students could even attend sermons in Italian at Mercers' Chapel in London. Some of the language teaching – such as Florio's *First Fruits* – is remarkably modern.[12] Florio's book starts with dialogue, and *then* gives grammar rules, and pays attention to the social identity of the speaker: this is a precursor of the communicative approach to language learning that is common today. Dialogues in Italian and English are presented in parallel columns, and cover topics related to everyday life and the joys (?) of travelling abroad, such as finding accommodation, dealing with landlords, wooing a gentlewoman, and ordering food.

Quando si parte la Posta?	When departeth the post?
Si dice domani	It is said tomorrow
Siatene certo?	Are you sure?
Non già io	Not I
Come lo sapete?	How know you that?
Lo ho sentito dire	I have heard it said
Dio vi dia il buon giorno	God give you a good morrow
Et a voi il buon giorno,	And to you a good morrow,
e buon anno	and a good year

… Which is a good deal more reasonable than a current CD-set of teaching Italian that includes a dialogue about finding the shoe factory.

---

cut short when he was hanged in 1554 after the death of King Edward VI, to whom he acted as a kind of tutor. His hanging, it seems, was not connected to his grammar book, although, given the attitude of the English to language learning, it would hardly have been surprising.

[12] John Florio (1553–1625) was pretty interesting too: he translated Montaigne's *Essays* into English and tutored Lady Jane Grey. He was *not* executed – unlike his mistress, whose life was (literally) cut short in 1554.

Florio uses proverbs and idioms as his sources for teaching colloquial Italian, and as a key to understanding the different ways that the English and Italians look at the world – something that we shall look at in the next chapter. (For example, the English see something that doesn't fit as a square peg in a round hole – the Italians see it as 'C'entra come i cavoli a merenda' ('fits like cabbage for the afternoon snack')).

PALACE ALERT: QUEEN ABOUT TO MAKE HER ITALIAN JOKE AGAIN!

Lord Robert Dudley, Earl of Leicester and one of the Chief Courtiers of Queen Elizabeth I, has warned the court that failing to laugh as loudly as usual at the Queen's favourite joke could be a capital offence. The Queen, greeting diplomats, likes to enquire whether they have seen beautiful things in England, and adds 'Se havete veduto cose, che vi siano piaciute, hora vedete il pegio, ch' è la patrona.' ('If you have seen things you liked, now you shall see the worst, that is, their mistress'.) Laughter at this point is now compulsory.

One can hardly blame her: Queen Elizabeth I spoke and wrote Italian very well – but making jokes in a second language is very difficult, so one joke can go a long way.

Queen Elizabeth II is, we are told, fluent in French. The President of Italy, Giorgio Napolitano, speaks impeccable English; David Cameron speaks halting French; among less reputable politicians, Silvio Berlusconi speaks French, which he perfected while working as a singer of romantic French songs in cruise ships, and Tony Blair also has passable French, which he learned while working in a bar in his GAP year.

But in Elizabethan and Jacobean days, Italian was useful and fashionable, and noblemen – and the Queen – would have been proud to be able to speak it. For example, when a group of noble Venetian travellers visited the English court in 1575 without any formal mission, they were nevertheless made very welcome and received at Windsor. One of them, Giovanni Falier, noticed that *quasi tutti* (nearly all) spoke Italian at the English court. Queen Elizabeth was proficient not just in writing official letters in Italian, but also in colloquial Italian, which she learned as a young lady (despite the fact that Roger Ascham had been one of her tutors!). When an official ambassador was sent by the Republic of Venice in 1603 to ask whether the queen would help the Venetians deal with the English pirates, she answered: 'Si, lo voglio far, et ve lo farò sapere, ma non so s'haverò ben parlato in questa lingua italiana, perchè io la imparai da fanciulla, credo che si, et non havermela scordata' ('I will, and I will let you know; but I do not know whether I have spoken this Italian language well; yet, since I learned it as a child, I believe I have not forgotten it.')

CLINT EASTWOOD ACCUSED OF UN-AMERICAN ACTIVITIES

Executives of United Artists have complained that Clint Eastwood has ruined their process of dubbing the 'Dirty Harry' films into Italian, because he speaks Italian already. When interviewed, Clint Eastwood said 'Coraggio, fatti ammazzare' ('Come on, let me kill you') which the United Artists executives claimed to be unfair use of an unlicensed foreign language.

Of course – it's not quite as simple as that.

The Italians love English – and they love English/American movies and TV series, but that does not mean that they are willing to listen to them in English. Everything is dubbed into Italian.[13] The English on the other hand – on the rare occasions when they can bring themselves to watch something 'foreign' – use subtitles. In fact, translations of *anything* into the English language are quite rare – only a tiny proportion of books and films in English are translations.

In Italy the result has been that the quality of the Italian 'voice actors' is outstanding, and may actually *improve* on the original. Very often the same Italian voice actor dubs the same foreign actor, so Ferruccio Amendola is Robert de Niro and Sylvester Stallone, Giuseppe Rinaldi is Paul Newman, and so on. One entertaining side effect is that as the same actors also do voice-overs for TV commercials, and so it is odd to hear Sylvester Stallone's voice advertising sanitary pads or Dustin Hoffman encouraging you to put more bran in your diet!

But for those brave few English who have attempted to learn Italian, or for those Italians who, having learnt English are still wondering how the English view of the world can be so linguistically perverse, let us turn to the way the different languages shape the world. Why on earth do the prudish English say 'You have made your bed now you must lie in it' while the lazy Italians say 'Hai voluto la bicicletta? Ora pedala!' ('You wanted a bicycle now you have to pedal')?

Why indeed!

---

[13] The Italian mania for dubbing goes back to Mussolini, who not only made the trains run on time (a strange anomaly in Italian behaviour) but who decreed in 1927 that to protect Italian culture and the Italian film industry, no foreign languages could appear on the screen. This was taken a step further in 1934 when films that had been dubbed abroad were banned – MGM and other American film-makers opened dubbing studios in Rome. Even Italians have been dubbed into Italian, notably Sophia Loren and Gina Lollobrigida when they were starting out. (Of course that wasn't just an Italian foible – the same thing happened to the American actress Andie MacDowell.)

Chapter 4

Speaking the World:

Idioms and World Views

Italians and English see the world in radically different ways.

Remember that the Italians invented the pianoforte and the violin, spectacles (around 1300: Petrarch was one of the first Italians to wear them) chiaroscuro and perspective, and the paperback (Aldo Manuzio in the 15th century).

And the English invented the steam engine, the National Health Service, cricket – and the mass-market paperback (Allen Lane – Penguin, 1935).

Countries who invent such different things structure the world differently and language is our way of structuring the world – of creating a world, even: we really perceive reality through language. As the linguist Ferdinand de Saussure has put it, 'Without language, thought is a vague, uncharted nebula'. In other words, language creates concepts.

For example, Italians don't have an equivalent for 'puppy fat': they still have fat children but you can't find, in Italian, *the concept* that fat may be part of childhood and that eventually children may grow out of it. In Italian children are just fat – they may lose the weight (or not!). Similarly, one of the words that is untranslatable from Italian into English is *abbiocco* – the sleepy feeling that you have after a large lunch: the English certainly have the feeling, but they do not have the word for it.

At the centre of language differences – and hence national differences – as we have seen, is the opposition between two words that are mutually untranslatable: *understatement* vs *bella figura*.

Understatement, the British way ('What did you think of the London Olympics?' asks the Italian; 'Not bad,' replies the Englishman) works by subtraction. It relies on irony and humour: it is a subtle, confident, and maybe snobbish way of seeing (or making) the world. It says: 'I can pretend I am less than I am because I know my worth!' Very English!

In contrast, *bella figura* (the closest translation is possibly 'making a good impression' – Beppe Severgnini translates it as 'making a good figure'[14]) is getting people to think that you are more interesting, intelligent, elegant, and wealthy than you are. It's performative, external, and about appearances: it's showing rather then being. It's what Italians do best (they are not too good at understatement, let's face it) and it may be fundamentally the result of insecurity. (It's not the same as the disparaging English expression 'all fur coat and no knickers' – meaning that somebody is *only* appearance and nothing else. The Italians have their knickers – they just want to make the best possible display of them. As it were.)

But these are BIG things about language – the devil, the fun, is in the detail. Take idioms – the pebbles of language that are so revealing of the way that we think. It might be easier if we were animals – even if Italian dogs say 'bau bau' rather than 'bow wow' and Italian cockerels say 'chicchririchi', rather than 'cock-a-doodle-doo they probably understand each other. But what are the English to make of a country that doesn't think that somebody is as thin as a rake, but as thin as an anchovy?!

Here's a story, translated literally from the Italian…

---

[14] Beppe Severgnini's *La Bella Figura – an Insider's Guide to the Italian Mind*, is the other essential book on Italy and the Italians (apart from this one). For him, 'La Bella Figura' is 'a sophisticated exhibitionism that has no need of an audience.' It's style, and it's in the blood.

THERE WAS ONE TIME
(AN ITALIAN FAIRY STORY)

There was one time, a young prince was in love with a local princess: he had slices of ham over his eyes ('fette di prosciutto sugli occhi') she was as cooked as a pear, and so their love was as smooth as oil. Then his potential mother-in-law said that the match was as inappropriate as cabbage for the afternoon snack ('cavoli a merenda'), because the Prince was missing a Friday, and he was as stiff as a salted cod. This insult was the last drop that made the vase tumble, and so the Prince and the Princess ran away, and despite having to organize a wedding serving dried figs, they were as happy as Easter ('felici come una Pasqua').

What?!!! Well, the English reader might be able to work out that 'missing a Friday' is the same as 'not the full shilling', or 'his lift doesn't go to the top floor' or a hundred other variants – or that the tumbling vase is the same as the camel's back – but surely lovers are blind because they have stars in their eyes, not slices of prosciutto on them (and once you have heard this image you can never watch prosciutto being sliced without this STRANGE image coming to mind). And dried figs? A treat when you can't afford anything better.

Of course, the English and the Italians share a lot of idioms (or *nearly* share them): we both put cherries on the top of our achievements, steal candy from babies ('E' facile come rubare le caramelle a un bambino'), get as full as an egg ('pieno come un uovo'), and think things are as soft as butter; our geese are silly and our moles are blind.

Others are pretty close: Italians in the sun turn as red as red peppers, rather than lobsters, empty their sacks rather than spill the beans, think of very fat people as mountains of lard rather than tubs of lard and touch iron ('toccare ferro') rather than wood. In England, many a good tune is played on an old fiddle – in Italy, 'Gallina vecchia fa buon brodo' ('an old hen makes a good broth'). And one swallow doesn't make a summer in England, and doesn't make a spring in Italy ('una rondine non fa primavera') (swallows having got there earlier, of course).

Sometimes there are definitely Italian nuances – the English see a mess as a fine kettle of fish – the Italians see a lasagne or a frittata. Italians get as stiff as a salted cod rather than a board. In England 'you can say that again', in Italy, 'you can say that louder' ('puoi dirlo forte'); in England good things come in small parcels, and in Italy good wine comes in small barrels ('il vino buono sta nella botte piccola').

ITALIAN CHEF MAKES OMELETTE WITHOUT BREAKING EGGS

'I wanted to do something that no English chef can do,' boasted Maurizio Pizzi. Unfortunately Signor Pizzi's attempt to keep his upper lip stiff at the same time failed, despite his specially starched moustache.

The etymologies of these expressions sometimes have surprising overlaps. In English 'once in a blue moon', meaning a rare event, had religious connections: an anti-religious pamphlet of 1528 reads:

> O churche men are wyly foxes [...] Yf they say the mone is blewe / We must beleve that it is true / Admittynge their interpretacion.

In Italy, the expression would be 'once in a Pope's death' ('Una volta ogni morte di papa').

IN ITALY THEY DON'T SAY...

As we might expect, there are plenty of idioms in English for which there is no Italian equivalent. For obvious reasons (as you will know if you have visited a *panetteria*) Italians don't say 'this is the best thing since sliced bread' (come to think of it, it is far from obvious why the English say this, given the rubberized consistency of sliced bread...); nor do they talk about red herrings... or people in glass houses. And they don't say, 'When in Rome...'

As far as the Italians are concerned, the English have a curious thirst for tea ('not my cup of tea', or 'storm in a teacup' – in Italian storms happen in simple glasses), and curious taste in puddings, which they over-egg, and test by eating (how else?). And, naturally, cricketing idioms, such as 'on the back foot', or 'sticky wicket' don't seem to have caught (as it were) on in Italy.[15]

IN ENGLAND THEY DON'T SAY…

One of the more mystifying Italian expressions for having made a mess is 'Fare un '48' (possibly as mystifying as the English equivalent, 'to make a right Horlicks of something' is to the Italians[16]). This mainly refers to 1848 as the year of revolutions in Europe – and Italy – and possibly from the failed attempt by Charles Albert of Piedmont-Sardinia to defeat the Austrians and unify Italy (he was defeated at the battle of Custoza in 1848).

Two of our favourites:

'Sei sempre in mezzo come il prezzemolo' ('you are always in the way – like parsley!') – referring to the extensive use of parsley in Italian cooking![17]

And mysterious 'Non parlare di corda in casa dell'impiccato ('don't mention rope in the house of the hanged man'). Perhaps the

---

[15] Although we should be careful here. The first cricket match in Italy was played in Naples in 1793, and A. C. Milan was originally the Milan Cricket and Football Club. Italy now has an international cricket team, administered by the Federazione Cricket Italiana.

[16] Horlicks is a malted milk drink (from 1874) much beloved of the English as a bedtime comfort drink. This is, however, irrelevant, as in this case it is merely a semi-punning-euphemism for 'bollocks', which means nonsense, or to make nonsense of something, or is just a general expletive. The fact that it was, in the 19th century a slang term for 'clergyman' may or may not be relevant.

[17] In the great English classic, Jerome K. Jerome's *Three Men in a Boat*, the equivalent of parsley is cheese: 'Cheese, like oil, makes too much of itself. It wants the whole boat to itself. It goes through the hamper, and gives a cheesy flavour to everything else there. You can't tell whether you are eating apple-pie or German sausage, or strawberries and cream. It all seems cheese. There is too much odour about cheese.'

closest the English have to this is the expression 'don't mention the war', which may have originated in a notorious episode of John Cleese's *Faulty Towers* in 1975. (This has become a family saying as much as a national one, just as some families, when faced with unexpected guest at a meal, will mutter 'FHB' – 'family hold back' – but this is not used nation-wide.)

PROSCIUTTO MAN RESCUED FROM CANAL

John Bull (21) blamed his book of Italian idioms when he fell into the Grand Canal in Venice after having draped slices of ham òver his sunglasses in order to impress his Italian (now ex-) girlfriend. 'I should have suspected something' said shopkeeper Alfredo Campari, 'when he asked for 200 grams of Prosecco.'

And idioms can be embarrassing.

WHEN IS A BIRD NOT A BIRD?
A Cautionary Tale

A friend of ours who taught English to a group of 18-year-old Italian boys (she was newly appointed to the job and not much older than they were), decided to devote a class to English idioms and tried to translate them literally. But before she even attempted to translate and explain the meaning of 'A bird in the hand is worth two in the bush' the boys started giggling and then laughing incontrollably so that it became really difficult to restore order – and she was never taken seriously again in that class.

(She tried to explain that it was the British equivalent of the Italian 'meglio un uovo oggi che una gallina domani' – 'better have an egg today than a chicken tomorrow'. But that was not much use, as 'bird' ('uccello') in colloquial Italian means – how can we put this delicately – penis.)

THE SAME BUT NOT QUITE…

The Italians say:

> …as mad as a horse (as we shall see when we get to the food section, Italians do not have the English reverence for the horse)
> …as good as bread
> …drinks like a sponge
> …as deaf as a bell
> …as ugly as hunger
> …as flat as a plank

and, of course, *as fit as a fish!*

ITALIAN ACTOR BREAKS LEGS

'I thought it was a tradition,' said Fabio Avenzi, after being arrested for attacking fellow actors with a sledgehammer in a London theatre. 'Everyone said it, so I thought it only the polite thing to do.'

The Italian equivalent would have been 'in bocca al lupo' – 'into the mouth of the wolf' – to which the response is 'Crepi il lupo!' ('let's hope the wolf dies').

The soul of a language, it has been said, is in its undercurrents, so what do we make of the souls of the English and the Italians when they produce ways of thinking about life like these:

English	*Italian*
...fell in love like a ton of bricks	è cotto (he is cooked – in love)
You can't have your cake and eat eat it	Non si può avere avere la botta piena e la moglie ubriaca (you can't have a drunken wife and full barrel)
keep mum	acqua in bocca (keep water in your mouth)
He spends money like water	ha le mani bucate (she/he has holes in hands)
...pulling the strings	avere le mani in pasta (having your hands in the dough)
... tit for tat	rendere pan per focaccia (to return bread for...bread)

Foreigners *are* Funny

On the whole the English take a benign view of Johnny Foreigner, but it might shock them to discover that what they would call 'French leave' is, in Italian, 'filasela all'inglese' ('to take English leave') – although the Polish and the French have exactly the same expressions – 'wyjść po angielsku' and 'filer à l'anglaise'.

The Italians don't have an equivalent of the rather offensive 'Dutch courage' (or 'French letters'), but 'to go Dutch' becomes 'fare alla Romana' ('to go Roman'). And while in England heavy smokers (used to) smoke like a chimney, in Italy, they 'smoke like a Turk' ('fumare come un turco').

These are 'audible' differences in the way we speak the world. The next chapter looks at the differences in the ways that we divide the world – spaces: personal space, class space, living space – some of which are visible and some of which are not.

Chapter 5

Headspace Or, Are the Italians Horizontal and the English Vertical?

With some Useful Tips on Page Three, Toothpicks, and Kettles

This is a chapter about things that start out as invisible differences. Spaces inside heads.

On the surface, as we have seen, England and Italy seem to be much the same: they have roads, cars, houses, people – they may look slightly different, have different styles of architecture, different kerbstones, and the people dress slightly differently[18], but basically they seem to be the same. However, inside, under the skin, things are organised very differently, and sometimes these break out in surprising ways. Here are two…

The Page Three Problem

'Page Three' in England means, notoriously, pictures of undressed young women in a certain tabloid newspaper. So an English visitor to Italy might be surprised to hear an Italian TV presenter on a serious programme say 'e adesso passiamo alla terza pagina' ('now we move on to the third page'). Traditionally Italian newspapers were organised with the 'leader' on the front page, news on the second, and cultural items on the third, and *la terza pagina* is still used to mean the

---

[18] Peter defers to Laura's conviction that Italians are born with a sense of style. Indeed, it is quite painful to watch her looking in the windows of provincial-town dress shops in England.

culture section, even if it may not be physically on page three nowadays.

Terza Pagina and Page Three

(Speaking of newspapers, have you noticed how Italian newspapers – especially local ones – contain a vast amount of information – almost as if Italians write as fast as they speak – compared with English ones?... Space is filled quite differently.)

And Married Names

The English probably have at the back of their minds the idea that Italy is a male-dominated society, so it is surprising to find that while English women, the day after their wedding (or the day before), hurry to change their email address so that they can use their husband's surname straight away, Italian women keep their maiden name. Not only do they keep it, but if you are an employee at any level, from the town council to a factory, to a hospital, or a university, it is actually *illegal* to use your married name in official documents. This is why it is sometimes difficult for English ladies to buy property in Italy – if they are using their husband's name, they have to provide lots of documents to prove who they are!

Even more surprising than that is the fact that wives have to sign their husband's passport applications (and husbands have to sign their wives') – and can refuse to do so! And if you have children who are underage, even if you are divorced or not legally married, you also need the signature of the mother/father of your children if you are applying for a passport. It's designed to ensure that one of the parents does not escape! On the other hand, in England, it is your doctor or some other professional who witnesses your signature: in Italy, your spouse must do it!

Is this what you'd expect from our stereotypes?

So, here is a theory: the English are uptight, upright and vertical, and the Italians are laid back to the point of being horizontal.

Take housing. The EU average for percentage of flats is 46%: in Italy it is 53%: even the urban aristocrats of past centuries wanted to live on one floor, hence the name *piano nobile* given to the best floor of a palazzo – the *noble* floor. The very rich in England also have flats – and, like flat caps, this is a trait they share with the very poor.

But in the UK flats make up only 17% of the housing stock – and 5% of those are conversions (only the Norwegians (11%) and the Irish (4%) have fewer flats). The Englishperson's home typically has several floors (Italians are often quite surprised to see a steep staircase when they open the door into an English house). As the German Prince Pückler-Muskau observed in 1830 when he visited England, 'English houses are all the same, the inhabitants being stacked one above the other like cheeses in a warehouse'. The Englishperson's home also has a garden, however minuscule, and many English are bemused by the amount of time Italian flat-dwellers spend indoors – wasting all that precious sun. If you look at the outside of any Italian hotel, you can tell which rooms are occupied by the English: they're the ones with open shutters, day and night. The Italians want to sleep in TOTAL darkness and the sun filtering through shutters is something that no one wants to experience!

Italians go outside to parks – but here's another paradox: Italian parks are generally MUCH dirtier than English ones. We have already seen that Italian flats tend to be cleaner than English houses (Italians are generally horrified by fitted carpets, especially in bathrooms). But for public spaces the individualism of the Italians seems to prevail over the sense of community. This is also one explanation for the corruption of Italian politicians: they have an individualistic, idiosyncratic view of the public good and a very personal interpretation of where public money should go.

Class: the Vertical Space

Of course, it's more than housing: the English are straight (up and down) in a different way – society is organised vertically.

We could spend a whole chapter – a whole book – on class – but it would be rather skewed because class is a Very Important Issue in England, and a Very Negligible One for Italians. Class is a way of ordering the world in layers and establishing connections and barriers.

It is extremely difficult to get average Italians to understand how class works in England. They don't understand that accent is a social marker: as George Bernard Shaw said in the 'Preface' to *Pygmalion*: 'It is impossible for an Englishman to open his mouth without making some other Englishman hate or despise him.' The English class system is terrifying and complex but every Englishperson understands it. Italy (Italians claim) does not perceive itself as a society based on class. (Although some of our informants, who come from parts of the South, like Naples, insist that there is some awareness of class – even, as in England, signalled by the use of dialect.)

Of all the things in this book, this subject is the one that has reduced its authors to mutual incomprehension. Peter disbelieves it: from the train windows, the working-class areas of any Italian city look obvious enough to him: to Laura, they are where the less-well-off live. Because Italians are not aware of class, they don't talk about it, and it is irrelevant to the way they judge people or make friends: they generally don't care about it. Italians do not moderate their regional accents, regardless of their wealth. Although some people say that the 'best' Italian is spoken by a Tuscan who has lived for many years in Rome, again, this has nothing to do with social class – it can apply to a Tuscan factory worker. Italians look seriously distressed when you tell them that the English even shop according to class. If you are upper-middle you buy your toilet paper at Waitrose, and if you are working class you buy *the same brand of toilet paper* at Tesco. At this point your average Italian is starting to think that you are pulling his or her leg (or as you would say in Italian, *che lo stai prendendo in giro* – that you are taking him/her around).

But 'twas ever thus, in England. In Charles Booth's *The Life and Labour of the People of London* (1889) there is a map of London in different colours and each colour is associated with a social class: black is the lowest, and indicates deprivation and occasional crime; dark blue stands for the very poor – and occasional work; light blue, the poor, 18 to 21 shillings a week; grey, mixed; pink, regular wages; red, the middle classes; and gold, upper-middle. The whole city is based on class, and areas are well separated, which prevents meetings between different social classes. Jane Austen was keenly aware of this long before Booth: in *Pride and Prejudice* (1813) Elizabeth Bennet tells Mrs Gardiner about the limited chances of Bingley meeting Jane in London:

> We live in so different a part of town, all our connections are so different, and, as you well know, we go out so little, that it is very improbable they should meet at all, unless he really comes to see her. 'And *that* is quite impossible; for he is now in the custody of his friend, and Mr Darcy would no more suffer him to call on Jane in such a part of London! My dear aunt, how could you think of it? Mr Darcy may, perhaps, have *heard* of such a place as Gracechurch Street, but he would hardly think a month's ablution enough to cleanse him from its impurities, were he once to enter it; and, depend upon it, Mr Bingley never stirs without him. (chapter 25)

And, of course, there is the famous exchange in Oscar Wilde's *The Importance of Being Earnest* (1895):

> *Cecily*: This is no time for wearing the shallow mask of manners. When I see a spade I call it a spade.
>
> *Gwendolen*: I am glad to say that I have never seen a spade. It is obvious that our social spheres have been widely different.

Italians – if pushed – will say that social structure is better defined by wealth than by class (there are not that many Dukes and Counts around and a lot have only courtesy titles) – but they don't use class to label each other. Class-based tastes in dogs or holidays or cars or supermarkets and class-based words (like napkin or serviette) are completely unheard of.

Indeed, classlessness is enshrined in law. The third Article of the Italian Constitution (which was promulgated in 1947 and was explicitly anti-Fascist and anti-authoritarian and puts the emphasis on economic and social rights) says that it is 'the Republic's duty to remove all social and economic obstacles which limit citizens' freedom and *equality*'. After having lived in a totalitarian state for 20 years (with a collusive monarchy to say the least), the *padri costituenti* (the Fathers of the Nation) wanted to make sure that the new state was democratic and that, at least on paper, everyone was equal.

But it wasn't always like that, as the irascible Tobias Smollett (a Scot, buried in Livorno) observed in his *Travels Through France and Italy* (1766):

> There is a considerable number of fashionable people at Florence, and many of them in good circumstances. They affect a gaiety in their dress, equipage, and conversation; but stand very much on their punctilio with strangers; and will not, without great reluctance, admit into their assemblies any lady of another country, whose noblesse is not ascertained by a title. This reserve is in some measure excusable among a people who are extremely ignorant of foreign customs, and who know that in their own country, every person, even the

most insignificant, who has any pretensions to family, either inherits, or assumes the title of principe, conte, or marchese. (Letter XXVII)

He did, however, note that even then (as we shall see when we come to consider food), these class-barriers were flexible: 'With all their pride, however, the nobles of Florence are humble enough to enter into partnership with shop-keepers, and even to sell wine by retail.'

A century later, this tendency had become an article of faith. The Italian children's classic *Cuore* (1886) is set in a day school where the rich, the poor, the Southerners and the Northerners must cooperate to build the new nation. In many post-unification Italian children's books interclassism is a theme and a goal. The difference between this and the English school story could hardly be more striking: without the exclusivity of the public school, with its hypersensitivity to class (and race), and without its snobbery, the whole genre would collapse. The occasional working-class scholarship lad or girl might make good – but that is precisely the point. Even the most famous private school in the world, Hogwarts, is riddled with class assumptions.

Such class-distinctions are still fostered across the English school system – unlike in Italy. As Beppe Severgnini has noted, the Italian state school system, and especially the *Liceo*, one of the best types of secondary schools, appears to be the glue that, despite everything, still binds the nation:

> Look at the students as they celebrate the year's end. The office worker's son is making a pass at the businessman's daughter and the doctor's girl is wandering off with the plumber's boy. It's a social achievement and we should be proud of it.

The Italians have the *Liceo* and the English have *Henry V*:

> We few, we happy few, we band of brothers;
> For he today that sheds his blood with me
> Shall be my brother; be he ne'er so vile,

This day shall gentle his condition…

As Jeremy Paxman pointed out in *The English*: 'In the hierarchical context of the late sixteenth century, it is an astonishing proclamation.' Indeed it is, but it was mere rhetoric then, and it would be mere rhetoric now.

Spaced Out

Everyone (except a few hopeful politicians) agrees that England is probably the most class-bound society in the world: even hugging and kissing are class-bound!

ITALIAN CATATONIC OVER KISSING PROBLEM

Iago Marchitello from Naples was rushed to hospital at Heathrow suffering from a suspected nervous breakdown. His fiancée, Jenny Smith from London, said 'My whole family was there and he couldn't work out which ones to kiss once, which ones twice, which three times, which to air-kiss, which to hug, which to shake hands with (and with one hand or two), which to nod to, which to pat on the shoulder or back, and which to ignore. I think he panicked.' Mr Marchitello was later arrested for patting a nurse.

Which leads us to the vexing question of personal space.

The Italians are kissers: they – and this means *everyone* – kiss on *both* cheeks. Kissing in the street is acceptable. It is normal for men to kiss men as a greeting. Italians, unlike the English, still display a lot of affection, in private and in public, towards children (no paedophile paranoia yet!). Kissing children (a lot) is OK, and so is getting children to kiss people they don't know very well if they are friends of their family. (Adults inflict this on children in England, but mostly they are apologetic about it – to the children.)

But things are getting even more extreme: a lot of Italians kiss *and hug* now – and, even worse, as far as the English are concerned, Italians are very tactile and a lot of people will actually touch you lightly when they speak to you – it's a part of gesticulation – to emphasis a point.

Of course this leads to a certain amount of confusion, notably among optimistic English males (of *any* age). We should emphasise that all this kissing is NOT on the mouth. That is confined to romantic relationships: Italians do NOT kiss babies, children, friends, or optimistic strangers on the mouth!

Language Spaces

Which makes it all the more perverse that the Italians use *language* to create a distance between people, they have two modes of address: the *Lei* (formal) and the *tu* (informal). People tend to move from *dare del Lei* to *dare del tu* more rapidly now than they used to do, but the distinction is still there, although young people instinctively use *tu* when introduced to their contemporaries. And it is not unheard of, after an argument or a break-up between co-workers, for one person to say to the other 'and from now on, you will have to use the *Lei* when talking to me.'

Equally, there are some occasions when Italians are more formal than the English might expect. For example, Italians will always say 'permesso' ('is it permitted?') when visiting someone for the first time, and many will keep saying 'permesso' even if they are entering a house they have been to several times[19].

---

[19] 'Permesso' is very useful when you need to make space for yourself: Italians don't say 'excuse me' – if you say 'scusi' when you are trying to get off the bus, people may think you are apologising: use 'permesso' and they will make way for you.

The English, on the other hand keep their distance through irony – that not-very-admirable device which keeps power and knowledge to itself. Perhaps, as some cultural critics have suggested, this is because the English are afraid – of each other. Italy, a nation of peasants until a century ago, has no self-esteem to be punctured. This might well account for why the English aren't as popular as they would like to think. A recent survey by VisitBritain, published in the *Daily Telegraph* (9th April 2014) listed Britain as a poor 16th in a list of 35 nations likely to offer the most friendly welcome. Not only were they thought to be arrogant and unfriendly, but the English sense of humour received the lowest score of any category and the Italians rated them as the second least funny people in the world!

We could write another book on the differences in non-verbal language – although the general opinion is that Italians have a great deal of it. Smollett called Italy 'the native country of hyperbole' and it certainly shows in the hands. The English gesticulate – but verbal vocabulary is spectacular: for example (to pick three from thousands), Italians pull the skin under their eye to show you that they are in the know, they rotate their index finger and point it towards the centre of their right cheek to tell you that what they are eating is delicious, and touch their waist on the right side with their flat right hand a couple of times to tell you that they are hungry. Cataloguing these gestures is not new: the first collection, *Gesture in Naples and Gestures of Classical Antiquity* (*La mimica degli antichi investigata nel gestire napoletano*) by Canon Andrea de Jorio was published in 1832.

Town and Country Spaces

When it comes to the layout of the countries, the stereotype would say that the vertical English are far more ordered than the horizontal Italians – but look at roads and towns.

Here is G. K. Chesterton, professional English eccentric, in *The Flying Inn* (1914):

> Before the Romans came to Rye
> Or out from Severn strode
> The rolling English drunkard

Made the rolling English road.

And then the proto-Italians came and straightened things.

Italians are addicted to their *autostrada* – toll motorways. They even give them names: not for the Italian driver the dull M25 or the A1(M) – they head North and South on the Autostrada 'del Sole' (A1), or to Trieste and back on the 'Serenissima' (A4). And they have 6661 km of autostrada to Britain's 3497 km of motorways. English towns (until very recently) were notoriously unplanned, whereas most Italian towns radiate out from their piazzas: even Italian railway stations always seem to be in much the same place relative to the town centres they serve. The English, if you look at the maps, seem to live in a state of relative disorder: compare the anarchic layout of the London tube system (402km of track, 270 stations) with the relative logic of the Milan metro (94.5km of track, 103 stations)!

TWO USEFUL TIPS FOR TRAVELLERS

These ways of looking at the world can defeat the most experienced travellers.

TOOTHPICK TRAPS UNWARY EATER
STUDENT SHUNNED FROM POLITE SOCIETY

Charles Smythe (20), a student, has returned home in disgrace from his academic year in Italy, and may have to abandon his degree, having failed one of the most subtle cultural tests. At the end of a meal, he took one of the toothpicks that were displayed prominently on the restaurant table – *and used it to pick his teeth*! Several sensitive Italian diners had to be treated for shock, and the *ristoratore* had to be restrained from suicide because of the shame of it all. Mr Smythe has now decided to become a monk.

This is really perverse!

Toothpicks are always on restaurant tables and many houses will put some on the table at the end of a meal and guests may be encouraged to use them. But you must be careful: it's a trap!!! Using a toothpick is considered very impolite, as in Italy is everything that has to do with putting your hands in your mouth during or after a meal. Many English people don't even realize that they are doing it, but will often remove bits of food from their teeth with their fingers at the end of a meal. This shocks Italians almost as much as the English are shocked by apparent greed (which Italians perceive as merely enjoying the food: enthusiastic eating is a compliment to the host). So don't let them trick you into using a toothpick: they have seen you clean your teeth, they are thinking 'the English have no manners' and the only reason why they are offering toothpicks to you is a test – they want to confirm their bad opinion of your table manners.

(For the record, well-behaved Italians would remove tooth-bound bits of food privately, when no-one is watching, generally in the bathroom – and some ladies carry dental floss in their handbags.)

And, of course, there are bidets and kettles…

Notoriously, the English do not know what to do with the bidet: they have washed their socks in them for generations. But before our Italian readers become too smug, we should consider the kettle. Not many people know that in the years before the kettle entered Italian houses (and even now, only a small percentage of Italians, generally Anglophile, have one in their kitchens) it was still an exotic appliance to be found with complimentary tea bags in many English bed and breakfast establishments. When Italian youths started touring England with InterRail, kettles were known to act as convenient scaled-down versions of washing machines. To wash socks!

Both the English and the Italians, then, have different subconscious concepts of space – but what happens when they come together in smaller spaces for parties and celebrations and rites of passage?

Chapter 6

Ceremonies and Holidays

There are few more cheerful sights than an English wedding spilling out of the lych-gate in a country village, with morning suits and big hats – or the smart but low-key clothes of Italian wedding-guests milling around a bright piazza. Italian churches stand four-square and Palladian in the centre of their towns or villages; English churches tend to lurk modestly among their yews and graveyards – but they are both symbolic of the rites of passage of the people – and of local traditions. Not surprisingly, the ways in which the English and the Italians navigate through life are full of happy and unexpected contradictions.

Hatching, Matching and Dispatching

England, it has to be admitted, is a pretty godless country. Around 800,000 people go to Church of England services each week – that's under 4% of the population: around 140,000 babies are baptised (20%)[20]; 55% of couples are not married – and of those who do get married, 70% choose civil ceremonies. Even when it gets to death, God is not that popular – only 34% of people choose (or are given) church funerals. Over 30% – and especially the young – claim to have no faith at all.

But, surely this can't be true in Italy, a good Catholic country where there seems to be a church or a shrine every kilometre in the country and a magnificent Duomo on every city corner.

---

[20] There has been a slight increase in infant baptism, for the unreligious reason that it increases the chances of eventually getting the child into a 'church school'.

After all, 90% of all Italians identify themselves as Roman Catholic – but despite the Vatican, the churches, and an amazing number of relics on display, even in the Veneto (traditionally the most Catholic of all regions in Italy) only 15% of people attend church every Sunday. In fact, Catholics are now a minority group in Italy – even women, traditionally the mainstay of the church, are falling away. A majority of babies are still baptized (70%), but in 2012, for example, registry office weddings outnumbered religious ones in the North of Italy, 52% (47% in the centre, only 23% in the South). But there is no law yet on civil partnerships or same-sex weddings: as often happens in Italy, society moves at a much faster pace than legislators.

To Begin at the Beginning

Italy has the lowest birth rate in Europe, and the number of couples living together outside marriage has doubled in the last few years, so we might reasonably assume that there are few who follow religious teachings in not using contraception or not having sex before marriage.

Italian weddings – 'Darling, Do you think 13 courses will be enough?'

What really surprises the English is that weddings in Italy, on average, are far less flamboyant than English ones.

Italians (and some English) are astounded to find that the *average* cost of a wedding in England is £18,000: there is an industry of wedding magazines, planners and the rest. The average wedding dress costs over £1000. Even the stag or hen parties cost over £150 *per head.*

Italians (in Italy, at least), do it more quietly. Stag and hen nights are rare – guests wearing hats are *extremely* rare, and flocks of bridesmaids and best men are replaced by simple 'witnesses', normally one person per spouse. They are not dressed differently from other guests – still no hats. Creamy colours are worn occasionally – although people at a wedding make a point of being elegant, it is not necessarily *wedding* elegant. Otherwise, the ceremonies, in church or in the Town Hall are much the same – although there are some striking small differences. In England the Bride and Groom lead the way out of the church, in Italy they may well be the last to leave, having been chatting to the priest or their family. In England there may be some cheerful confetti throwing (usually biodegradable stuff, so as not to ruin the churchyard paths); in Italy, friends have been sighted waiting with 10 kilo sacks of rice for the bride and groom to emerge.

So if Italians don't really care much about wedding planners, and are not obsessed with themes, colour schemes or the perfect décor, can we assume that the emphasis is on the couple, and on the celebration of the union?

Wrong.

The most important thing in an Italian wedding is the quality – and the quantity – of the *food*. The typical question that you may be asked after attending a wedding is 'Hai mangiato bene?' ('did you eat well?'). Wedding dates are often decided on the basis of the availability of a good restaurant, and most couples spend many happy evenings sampling menus in advance. It must be the legacy of centuries of peasant starvation, but at an Italian wedding you *always* eat too much; the number of courses is generally ridiculous – it is often the case that the more homely the wedding is, the more delicious the food will be, with even more courses than usual.

Here is a real (fish-themed) menu from a wedding reception in Northern Italy.

Aperitivo in Portico

Antipasti
Nidi di polenta con Gamberetti fritti
Antipasto al vapore
Capa Santa – Cape Lunghe alla griglia

Primi Piatti
Risotto alla marinara
Garganelli all' Astice
Gnocchi al granchio

Sorbetto

Secondi Piatti
Branzino di mare in bella vista
Scampi e mazzancolle – Seppie alla griglia
Frittura di Paranza
Insalata mista – Patatine fritte

Sorbetto al limone
Dolce degli Sposi – Spumante
Caffé

Il tutto accompagnato da Vino Prosecco

And this is not a choice!

We were going to translate this gastronomic poem, with its opening rhapsody of such things as polenta nests with friend shrimp, scallops, razor clams, pasta with lobster, and crab gnocchi. But as the guests would have enjoyed their *Aperitivo* in the entrance hall, and as everything was *accompagnato da Vino Prosecco*, it seemed that after a while, translation would be irrelevant. After all, a poem, as Archibald MacLeish observed, 'should not mean, but *be*.'

Best men don't make speeches, dancing is not *necessario* ('*de rigueur*' as we would say in English) and the meal may last for four or five hours. Some couples even organize two separate wedding receptions – a meal with just the family members for lunch (most ceremonies being in the morning) and dinner with friends in the evening, but the BIG LUNCH where people mix is probably still the most popular. And not all guests will end up drunk – the most common toast is simply the crowd shouting 'Bacio, bacio!' – no-one, apparently ever has enough of seeing the couple kissing!

But... Funerals are Funerals

In England, a funeral usually involves a party: an ambiguous party, perhaps, but a 'send off', or an appreciation or a celebration of a life. At least, a few drinks: the Irish, of course, are notorious for the exuberance of their wakes – the English, being more restrained are, naturally... more restrained. Although here is a Yorkshire example:

> When I turn up my toes...
> I want no great wet weepings... no sad adieus;
> Go and get the priest and then – go get the booze, boys.
>
> Have a knees-up, shake it up, live it up, sup it up hell of a
> kind of a time,
> And if the coppers come around, well tell them – the party's
> mine...
>
> – *Jake Thackray,* 'Last Will and Testament'

And the Italians?

There is a joke:

An elderly Italian man lay dying in his bed. While suffering the agonies of impending death, he suddenly smelled the aroma of his favourite ravioli wafting up the stairs. He gathered his remaining strength, and lifted himself from the bed. Gripping the banisters with both hands, he crawled downstairs.

When he reached the bottom of the stairs, he leaned against the door frame, gazing into the kitchen, where if not for death's agony, he would have thought himself already in heaven. For there, spread out upon waxed paper on the kitchen table, were hundreds of his favourite ravioli.

Was it heaven? Or was it one final act of love from his wife of 60 years, seeing to it that he left this world a happy man? He threw himself towards the table, landing on his knees in a crumpled heap. His parched lips parted, the wondrous taste of the ravioli was already in his mouth.

With a trembling hand he reached up to the edge of the table, when suddenly he was smacked with a wooden spoon by his wife who said:

'Questi sono per il funerale' ('These are for the funeral').

Funny as this joke might be – note that it is *not* a translation from Italian – it is, quite simply, *not true*. Italians, food-obsessed as they are, don't eat at funerals. The dead are buried quickly, after two or three days maximum (they are not kept in fridges), and the funeral is a short affair: there is a Mass and then only the close relatives follow the coffin to the cemetery, where the priest says a few final words. Everyone kisses the bereaved and scurries home – the idea is that at such a sad moment you only want to be with your closest family members, and you must be exhausted anyway, and there will be time to get together later. It is a bit like Italian hosts *not* filling their guests' wine-glasses every five minutes (more about pouring in

76

Chapter 9) – it's about giving space to the other person to grieve, or drink, at leisure. Which, in a country where people keep touching each other all the time and don't really have a sense of personal space, shows remarkable restraint.

Rites of Passage

GAP years, 18th and 21st Birthdays, and Graduations.

Since 1884, 60% of male householders in England over 21 have been able to vote – in 1918 this was extended to virtually all males, and in 1918 to females over 30. For generations of the English, your 21st birthday was symbolic of adulthood (the song '21 today!' with the line 'I've got the key of the door/Never been 21 before' dates from 1911); in 1970, when the voting age was reduced to 18, the celebration shifted, although the 21st birthday celebration has not died out.

In Italy, this doesn't happen – 18 and 21 are not particularly important – and, as we have seen the GAP year is a novelty. Mandatory military service, another key rite of passage for a generation has also become a thing of the past although it survived longer in Italy: 'National Service' ceased in 1960 in England, but not until 2005 in Italy.

But there is one event that stands out as a new rite of passage each year for around 337,000 students in England, and 388,000 in Italy: university graduation. The biggest difference is in the award of Masters' Degrees – in England candidates graduate *en masse* once a year, with fairly low-key celebrations. In Italy, you graduate when you have finished writing your dissertation, and MA vivas are public: the candidate's family and friends will go to the viva and listen to the discussion, often not understanding anything that is going on. But they are invariably very elegant, and look appreciatively around at the *Aula Magna* (the best room of any university is invariably used for graduation vivas) smile proudly at the professors who are examining the candidates, and send silent messages such as 'I am the grandmother, you know'. The candidate does not wear a gown. After discussing his or her thesis, he or she graduates on the spot, is given a laurel wreath to wear, and everyone celebrates with a meal and a wild party. Which can be *very* wild.

One oddity for the English is that Italians do not send birthday or Christmas cards – apart from small cards that accompany the ubiquitous small presents. The positively baroque greetings-card shops that adorn the high streets of England, or the huge card sections in bookshops, or in W. H. Smith's are simply unknown.

It is considered polite by the Italians to open presents that they are given, immediately, so that they can thank the giver. Not for them the English dilemma of trying to match card to gift after the guests have departed!

Festivals and Festivities

TURKEY DETECTORS ROAM ENGLISH STREETS BEFORE CHRISTMAS

The English Christmas is now being enforced by advanced TDT – Turkey Detection Technology. In the days leading up to Christmas, any householder who cannot prove that they have a large dead bird and a copy of *A Christmas Carol* in the house will be convicted of un-English activities and be forced to eat spaghetti for the whole of January. A plea of 'will roast beef do?' will be considered by magistrates. Turkey burgers are inadmissible.

Like much else about festivals and food in England, Christmas has become homogenised. Around 10 million turkeys (or about 15,000 tonnes) are eaten, and probably the same number of Christmas puddings. Together with bread sauce, cranberry sauce, roast potatoes and stuffing. Santa Claus/Father Christmas comes down the chimneys with the presents during the night of Christmas Eve. Eight million Christmas trees are decorated. There may be minor variations, but the curious hotch-potch of traditions that make English Christmases, laden with pseudo-nostalgia and pseudo-snow has congealed into a curiously uniform, highly commercialised secular celebration (advertising for which begins around July).

Needless to say, the Italians cannot agree on Christmas food – apart from *panettone* (originally from Milan), *pandoro* (originally from Verona), and *torrone* (originally from Cremona). In some places, more emphasis is put on the *cenone della vigilia* (the evening meal on Christmas Eve) than the actual Christmas lunch. Generally the *cenone* is based on fish – for example, fried *capitone* – a large eel – in Naples, *bigoli* with sardines by Lake Garda; fish soup in Rome, etc.). The *pranzo di Natale* (Christmas lunch) is based on meat – *tortellini* and *bolliti* – a selection of boiled meats – in Bologna; roast lamb in Sardinia; capon in Bergamo and so on. But these are multi-course meals, with lots of vegetables and sweets and cakes from local traditions.

Unfortunately there doesn't seem to be an agreement on who brings the presents either – mostly Father Christmas/Baby Jesus but not exclusively. For example, in Verona and Mantova it is St Lucy who brings the presents on December 13th while in Trieste and Belluno (and other places as well) it is Saint Nicholas, who on 6th December brings presents (but, curiously, not in Bari, where the saint is buried).

And then there is *La Befana*, an old crone who delivers gifts to children on the Epiphany (6th January). She looks more like a pantomime witch: she has, by consensus, a crooked nose and broken shoes – she flies all over Italy on her broomstick and carries a big bag on her back full of sweets, which she will use to fill the stockings children have left by the chimney, or by the Christmas tree. The bad children are threatened with having lumps of coal instead.

In contrast, while England (as opposed to Scotland) doesn't seem to have made up its mind about New Year's Eve, Italians go for another *cenone della vigilia*. This time (with inevitable regional variations) lentils seem to be a staple – symbolising or good luck with money (a bit like wearing red knickers on New Year's Eve, for good fortune in... another area!).

A Year Of Festivals

The Italians say 'Natale con i tuoi, Pasqua con chi vuoi' ('spend Christmas with your family, and Easter with whoever you want') – and the Italian calendar is peppered with festive days.

After La Befana, and before Ash Wednesday, there's Carnival. The English are very sloppy about this – 'Carnival' in Italy is the pre-lent celebration when all the rich food was consumed – a very ancient tradition on the Italian peninsula. In England, all that is left of this tradition is Shrove Tuesday, when flour, eggs and milk are used up to make pancakes – and English 'Carnivals' occur throughout the year. In Italy, Carnival means every town having different celebrations (such as the procession of floats in Viareggio) and different foods. Children dress up for Carnival (and some adults too) traditionally as *commedia dell'arte* characters (like Pulcinella, or Arlecchino), but more recently as superheroes, or princesses, or fairies, or famous people. Children go out in their costumes and and throw confetti (*coriandoli*, in Italian) at each other in Italian piazze, or go to parties.

Bank holidays in England are on fixed days of the week, whereas in Italy several religious and civil holidays have fixed *dates* and so can fall on any day of the week. These include 1st May (The workers' day), 25th April (the fall of Mussolini's Italian social Republic and the end of the Nazi occupation in Italy in 1945) or 8th December, the Feast of the Immaculate Conception. This means that long weekends may or may not happen, so Italians have adopted the bridge system ('il ponte') – when a holiday occurs on a Tuesday or a Thursday, the gap between the holidays can be filled by an extra holiday. People ask for that gap day off work in order to have a long weekend, and sometimes schools will close on that gap day. (The closest the English get to this is the bridge – or rather, viaduct – between Christmas and New Year, a gap that is too short to work in and too long to holiday in.)

Italy still has a vestige of what in England used to be called 'Wakes Weeks' – the summer holiday periods when whole towns and regions went on holiday together. This is *Ferragosto*, 15th August (the Assumption of the Virgin Mary) and as it is at the height of summer most Italians traditionally get out of the cities and head for the beach or the mountains. Although now most Italians will have their holidays at other times, traffic jams and accidents are still a feature of travelling on the *ponte di Ferragosto* – the *esodo di Ferragosto* (the Ferragosto Exodus) epitomises everything that the English fear about Italian driving.

Now… throughout this book, we have been very careful to avoid, or explode, obvious prejudices and stereotypes, but when it comes to Italian driving, we are going to have to make an exception. Many traumatised English drivers in Italy will testify that, to put it kindly, Italians take their natural exuberance onto their roads. The English, by and large, exercise their natural diffidence and politeness in their cars: a visibly significant number of Italians use their cars as expressions of personal freedom and total fearlessness. Of course, even the mad drivers are good at mad driving, otherwise there would be carnage – and the English might be surprised to find that Italy has only marginally more road fatalities than England (7.6 per 100,000 cars as compared to 6.2). And Italians can surprise other Italians. Last year, caught in a traffic jam on the way to Milan's Malpensa airport, we watched a driver on the other side of the road parking in a space just too small for his car, by the simple expedient of shunting backwards and forwards until the space was big enough. Our taxi driver merely shook his head.

(And the less said about Italians and roundabouts, the better.)

Patron Saints and Village Fairs

The English Tourist Board, that skilled purveyor of fantasy, may be partly responsible for the rapid increase in English local fairs and festivals – literary festivals and beer festivals being perhaps the most common. There is, of course, the deeply ingrained tradition of the village fête, purely local and unprerentious affairs. But there are many pleasantly eccentric examples, such the Ramsbottom Black-

Pudding throwing championships, the Welly-Wanging championships at Upperthong in Yorkshire, or the (rather more lethal) Cheese Rolling at Cooper's Hill in Gloucestershire. Not surprisingly there are games with purely satirical origins, such as Dwyle Flonking from Norfolk.

On the whole, the Italians take their Patron Saints' Days and Fairs more seriously, to the extent that almost every local dish or produce or vegetable must have its moment of glory, its celebration and its village fair. You can do a gastronomic tour of Italy through its village fairs, or *sagre*, from the 'sagra dello Stufato d'Asino' ('donkey stew') in Calliano, Piedmont, to the 'Cous Cous Fest' in Trapani, Sicily; from the 'Sagra del Sedano' (celery) in Bassano, Veneto to the 'Panettone Party' in Rieti, Lazio, which, very bravely, is held on Ferragosto. There are fairs for frogs (several), fish, all kinds of salami, vegetables (from asparagus to chicory, from truffles to peppers), fruit, cakes, pasta, eggs, birds, all sorts of meat, polenta, tortellini, clams, wine, olives, chocolate...

Some of the names of these food village fairs are in the local dialect. For example, in Gignod, Valle D'Aosta, in August they have the 'Feta di teteun' – very difficult to decipher by anyone not speaking the local dialect (just as well, as the 'teteun' is a special dish made with cows' udders). Near Trento, in the small village of San Lorenzo in Banale (1168 inhabitants) they have the 'Sagra della ciuiga' – the *ciuiga* being a very unusal sausage invented in the second half of the 19th century, made with pork and white turnips, and then smoked. And on sale only in that village.

And there are political hangovers: *Festa de l'Unità* is a summer celebration originally organised by the Italian Communist Party to finance and spread its official newspaper *l'Unità*, and now organised by Partito Democratico. In some parts of Italy, especially in Emilia Romagna and Tuscany, where the leftist party has a majority, every village or city seems to have its own 'festa de *l'Unità*' with cheap food, grills, street markets – and usually an opportunity for ballroom dancing in the open.

'In the open' being the key... The English climate is perhaps not so conducive to *al fresco* activities – although it is worth pointing out that when the Italians say *al fresco* they don't mean what the

English mean by it! 'Fresco' just means 'cool' in Italian so *al fresco* can be anywhere where there is a nice, pleasant temperature (often, a nice air-conditioned place *inside*).

Chapter 7

Matters of Sex and Gender (Some Serious)

Of course, we all know that

– Italian men are Macho – except for the ones who live at home with their mothers. Recently, an Italian marriage was annulled because the husband had 'a mother fixation'

– the English don't have sex lives (they have hot-water bottles) and the lusty, lively Italians are excitingly uninhibited and go to bed with (or at) a drop of Armani scent.

So it would seem that in matters of sex and gender, the Italians and the English are worlds apart…

Well, not exactly.

Babes, Birth rates and Breastfeeding

In many ways, the two countries are in step. In both countries

– Women are overtaking men as graduates and as doctors – and girls have better exam results than boys.

– Women are waiting longer to have their first child; birth rates are low, but despite what the English might expect, they are lower in Italy than England (1.4 to 1.9 babies per woman) and Italy has one of the lowest rates of infant mortality in the world.

But

– the average life-expectancy is much the same (Italy 82, England 81.5)

– the number of women in top jobs remains small – there is still a glass ceiling

and

– female salaries are lower.

It might seem that Italian women do better in politics: 20% of British MPs are female as opposed to 30% in Italy – and while England still has token female cabinet ministers, 50% of Italian ministers are women.

But underlying this fairly meagre proportional success is, in both countries, a deeply sexist problem. Berlusconi was accused of degrading the credibility of female politicians by appointing women to political positions for questionable reasons. Mara Carfagna, his Minister for Equal Opportunities 2008-11, the media could not resist pointing out (variously), had been a 'topless model' and 'showgirl' – and number one on *Maxim's* list of 'The World's Hottest Politicians'. Even a respectable, professional politician, Elena Boschi, Minister of Constitutional Reforms since 22 February 2014, has had a viral picture (photo shopped) of her signing an act while exposing her thong.

All very well, but female MPs in England are routinely harassed and demeaned in the House of Commons by what is seen widely as a regressive male club. The 101 female Labour Party MPs of the 1997 election (under 20% of the whole house and there were only 19 others from all the other parties) were paraded as 'Blair's Babes'. In the 2014 Conservative-Liberal Democrat cabinet reshuffle the eight female members (out of 28) were called 'Cameron's Cuties' and several papers ran fashion profiles of them.

HISTORIC ITALIAN-ENGLISH ANTI-SEXIST ACCORD

At today's ceremony, intended to wipe out sexism in Italian and English politics, the treaty was signed by Signor Rocco Manzan and Sir Roderick Spode. Signor Rocco (46) pert father of five, with smart grey tints in his dark hair, was dressed in a grey Canali suit with open-necked white shirt revealing his deep tan; Sir Roderick (46-56-59), hair by Brigante of Chelsea, titillated the other ministers with a glimpse of his Marks and Spencer's underpants as he leaned over the desk. Complaints from female ministers that the media had focussed on trivia, were dismissed as trivial.

This kind of veiled oppression is hardly funny, though. A survey by the *Daily Mail* in September 2014 showed that breastfeeding in public was still widely taboo in England. In Italy, it is more acceptable – but when an Italian MP complained that she couldn't breastfeed in parliament, very few women commentators were sympathetic. The subtext was that you can't have it all, that being an MP is a privilege, and that you have to make sacrifices if you want such a good job. Men's comments were even more dismissive: if you want to breastfeed, stay at home!

Se non ora, quando?
(If not now, when?)

Here are some statistics that might seem startling to both the English and the Italians.

– In England, women (over 30) got the vote in 1918: in Italy it was in 1946.

– In England, brothels were outlawed in 1885 – in Italy *State* brothels were closed down in 1958 ('la legge Merlin' – 'Merlin's law' after Lina Merlin, a socialist senator). This was after nine years of fighting in the Italian parliament, and even then male public opinion was divided, for brothels were believed to be a way of ensuring that the family would stay together – an attitude that in England lingered barely into the nineteenth century.

– In 1950s Italy, adultery was punished by prison – but only *female* adultery. (The last woman to be punished by law for adultery (she was hanged) in England was in 1654.)[21]

– In 1963 it became illegal to sack a female worker in Italy who got married. But just in case any of our English readers are feeling superior, the same laws were still in force in parts of the English civil service until the late 1960s.

– Homosexuality was decriminalised in England in 1967 (in the Isle of Man in 1992), whereas in Italy the code Zanardelli decriminalized sexual intercourse between consenting adults above the legal age of consent in all regions of Italy *in 1889*. In the regions using the Code Napoleon, roughly the South of Italy, it had been legal for decades.

Many things in this area are much the same – for example, abortion was legalised in England in 1967, in Italy in 1978 – but some things are radically different. In England, the first case of an 'honour' killing by someone not belonging to a specific ethnic immigrant group was reported in 2013. In Italy, until 1981 *il delitto d'onore* – a murder performed to save one's own honour (as in the case of a husband killing a wife who had an extramarital affair) – was punished with a very light sentence (from three to seven years).

---

[21] The big Italian scandal of the 1950s was the adulterous relationship of the champion cyclist Fausto Coppi (who won the Giro d'Italia five times and the Tour de France twice) with Giulia Occhini, called *la Dama Bianca* (*The Woman in White*) who was married to an army officer. They moved in together and the police raided their house to check whether they were sleeping together: *even the Pope* asked Coppi to return to his wife! Giulia was sent to prison for a few days and was under house arrest for months. Coppi's career declined after the scandal (his passport was confiscated), and spectators spat at him during the races.

Another typically Italian institution which survived until 1981 was that of the *matrimonio riparatore* (rehabilitating marriage): according to the Italian Code of Criminal Procedure of the time, if a rapist offered to marry his victim, he would have his crime automatically extinguished. Traditional social conventions decreed that a woman would lose her 'honour' if she did not marry the man she lost her virginity to. Until 1981 rape was considered a crime against public morality rather than a personal offence. The greatest influence on changing the law was possibly not the feminists, but the case of Franca Viola, a Sicilian farmer's daughter, who publicly refused to marry her rapist, a local Mafia boss, in 1965, and appealed to the law to prosecute the rapist. As a consequence, her family were persecuted and her cottage and vineyard were burned to the ground. But her trial had a wide resonance in the Italian media, and it became obvious that the article of the law clashed with public opinion. The trial found the rapist guilty – he was condemned to 11 years in prison. Franca, who then married the man she loved in 1968, became a symbol of women's emancipation in post-war Italy, and many women refused the 'matrimonio riparatore', following her example.

Rape has been a crime in England since the 17th century.

The attitudes behind all this may account for some of the differences in the ways that the feminist movements in Italy and England have developed.

PAGE THREE WARS: THE BATTLE OF THE SEXISTS

Since 1970 the English tabloid newspaper *The Sun* has been running 'page three' images of 'topless' young women (with a spectacular effect on its circulation) and there have been long-running campaigns against them. Currently the website 'No More Page 3' cites such soft porn as contributing to '300,000 women being sexually assaulted and 60,000 raped each year' and that one in four of all women has been sexually assaulted (the figure for Italy is one in three). But this has not been taken seriously by the media: an anti-page three petition has (at the time of writing) 173,198 signatures – against 11 million weekly *Sun* readers. However, it seems possible that these consciously anachronistic images might well disappear as the newspaper needs more female readers to maintain its circulation.

Now compare Italy.

In 2009 Lorella Zanardo produced a hugely successful documentary, *Il corpo delle donne (Women's Bodies)*, on the grotesque exploitation of females on the Italian commercial TV channels, owned by Berlusconi. Zanardo has taken the film around Italy to schools and universities to make young people aware of the daily exploitation of the female body in media and culture, and it seems that Italian women have had enough. In February 2011 a movement called 'Se non ora, quando?' (from the title of Primo Levi's novel of 1982) called all women to action, and millions of women marched in cities and villages nationwide, carrying banners reading 'Italy is not a brothel'. For many women (and men), this was the first time that they ever demonstrated in the streets. You could see nuns and feminist organizations that oppose the Roman Catholic Church march side by side with housewives, right-wing female politicians and left-wing students. Since then, *Se non ora, quando?* has become a network of organized committees that works to keep attention focussed on women's demands.

EVEN DARKER SUBJECTS

One of the burning issues in Italy is *femminicidio* (femicide): there are almost daily headlines – 'wife killed by husband': in the first six months of 2014, 153 women were killed by their husbands, partners, or ex-husbands and ex-partners. That is more than one third of the murders reported. In England, the figure is one every three days, about 100 in the same period.

As often happens in Italy, laws seem to lag behind changes in society. Stalking became a crime in Italy only in 2009, and Italy started passing new Anti-Domestic Violence measures only in 2013, after what was called 'the gender war' by the journalist Riccardo Iacona in his book *Se questi sono gli uomini* ('If these are men' – a pun on the title of Primo Levi's novel *If this is a Man*). This is a war in which men arm themselves against women. And so domestic violence is still at epidemic levels in both countries: there are not enough shelters or safe houses to protect Italian or English women from abusers. Iacona's survey suggested that the Italian murderers were incapable of coping with women who are self-reliant, more educated and often the only breadwinners in the family, women who juggled a job and domestic work. The contribution by Italian men to domestic chores is among the lowest in Europe.

These tropes of patriarchal structures continue: in 2013 a parish priest from Turin sparked outrage with his Christmas bulletin board on which he declared that 'modern women's independence, arrogance, and not keeping a tidy house' were the reason for the rise in femicide. Femicide is now one of the top issues on the national agenda, as it has long been established that domestic violence is more prevalent than any other kind of violence in Italy. Campaigns are trying to combat domestic violence, and psychologists and sociologists are trying to explain the phenomenon in terms of an unresolved 'Men's Question'. This is the problem of men who are illiterate in the language of feelings, incapable of changing or adapting their roles in the family, or reacting rationally when they are rejected or left alone.

The English may suspect that femicide is connected to class: the Italians think there is something wrong with male identity, so they are not dismissive and they don't have the attitude 'it would never happen to us who are nice and middle-class'. What is the real Italy, one wonders? Is it the Italy of educated women, who can divorce, have an abortion, become MPs, judges or doctors? Or, according to the latest report by the National Institute of Statistics, the country where 31,9 % of all Italian women between 16 and 70 (6,743 million) have been victim of violence at least once in their lives?

But let us return to more cheerful, if not more puzzling, things....

THE *ALBERTO* REPORT

(**Cert: PG**: contains explicit references to underwear and personal hygiene and other topics unmentionable by the English)

> 'Contrary to popular belief, Englishwomen do not wear tweed nightgowns' – *Hermione Gingold*

But what *do* people in Italy and England wear in bed? It's fairly fundamental (as it were). And how on earth do we find out?

Kate Fox, in *Watching the English* had the same problem: 'Looking back at my research notes', she said, 'I was continually struck by the difficulty of having any sort of sensible conversation with English informants. The English simply cannot talk about sex without making a joke of it.' The Italians, at least in this, are not so inhibited, and we sent our fearless native investigator, Alberto, to find out what Italians do!

We asked Alberto to find out – after one of those twilight conversations in a piazza in among Italian friends, lubricated by Prosecco and powered by Prosciutto – whether Italians wear underwear in bed. His reply was: do the *English* wear underwear in bed? According to all the stereotypes, they obviously do!

But the true answer, according to the *Daily Telegraph* no less (10th April, 2014) is: that the English are twice as *less* likely to wear underwear in bed than the Italians. The results of a survey showed that the Britons were far more likely to forgo fusty passion-killing pyjamas and sleep naked in bed than their continental counterparts. …The British view of what to wear between the sheets is in sharp contrast to the Italians!

Alberto's research backed this up. He interviewed 50 Italians, aged 16 to 74, and with just one exception (a woman of 42, who didn't wish to answer – but she had lived abroad for most of her life and must have gone native) everyone admitted quite happily to wearing underwear in bed, under all circumstances (Alberto asked whether they removed it under some circumstances, like in hot weather).

They were horrified at the way in which the English behave: according to the Italians, it is not hygienic to go to bed without underwear (and lots of people wanted to know how often the English change their sheets). The English, in contrast, think that going to bed *with* underwear is unhygienic – and probably wonder how often the Italians change their underwear. Italian women wear underwear to protect themselves; whereas if English women wear underwear, it is to protect the bed.

And while we are in such dubious territory, let us briefly consider the bidet once again.[22] In England, the bottom, as it were, has dropped out of the bidet market, apparently bathrooms are smaller than they used to be – B and Q sell barely, as it were, 500 per year. Italians, in contrast use the bidet, it would seem, whenever possible, and must pity the English who never experience the small bidet-side towel or jar of pH neutral 'detergente intimo'.

Naturally, Italians like (or are obsessed with) clean underwear; most Italian men use scent, own twice as many suits as their English counterparts (who own three), are careful about colour coordination – and think that the way that the English macho man shows off his hairy stomach, is a joke!

---

[22] As this is the third time that we have mentioned the bidet in this book, we would not like you, Dear Reader, to think that we are in any way preoccupied with this object. We are mere amateurs compared with Paola Guagliumi who seems to have written a whole book on English behaviour in this area: *Perchè gli inglesi non usano il bidet* (*Why the English don't use the bidet*) (2001).

The English (like the Italians) have an expression – to wash one's dirty linen (that is, underwear) in public – which often refers to the English press's prurient interest in the private lives of public figures. The general attitude seems to be that taking public office means that you automatically sacrifice personal privacy. If David Cameron or, for that matter, Prince William are prepared to parade their families for political or publicity purposes, then they have in effect, signed a pact with the devil. Italians, in contrast, could not care less about politicians' personal lives or their spouses. Not much is known of wives or husbands of ministers and presidents – some Italian Presidents' wives don't even move to their official residence, the Quirinale. For example, the wife of President Sandro Pertini, one of the most popular presidents of all time (1978-1985), a resistance man and a socialist, worked as a psychiatrist in a hospital. She was never seen at the Quirinale, nor did she accompany her husband on any official engagements. And people just left her alone.

It is therefore ironic to think that the word 'Paparazzi' is Italian – coined by Federico Fellini in *La Dolce Vita*.

But from these intricate matters let us move on to the heart – the essence – of our book: food!

Chapter 8

Cibo dell'Anima – Soul Food

Or, How Can You Have Civilisation without Marmite?

A friend of ours recently returned from Italy, traumatised.

'They may have Tintoretto and the Coliseum, but they *don't* have Jelly Babies! Or...' (he gathered himself) '... hot buttered toast, Jaffa cakes, Ribena, custard, bacon – well, they do have a sort of bacon – they call it *pancetta*, poor things – but they chop it up into little cubes, would you believe – black pudding, digestive biscuits, bread and butter pudding, ginger cake, scones, roast beef, gravy, faggots, chips, Marmite... or large, fatty *proper* breakfasts.'

Italian Breakfast versus English Breakfast

Of course, an Italian might think that the above list sums up everything that's wrong with English eating – but would be too polite to say so. The English breakfast is only too evident on early morning trains in England, where everyone smells faintly of stale fat. [23]

GASTRONOMIC SCANDAL! ITALIANS EAT WORMS

And worse than *worms* (vermicelli)! They also eat *partridge's eyes* (occhi di pernice) and *priest stranglers* (strozzapreti). 'This is no more than we expected,' said Mrs Smith of Leicester. 'We have brought our own sliced loaves with us, and they are still fresh after a week. It is a tribute to the Leicester bakery.'

'But,' we said, 'think of all the wonderful food there is in Italy.'

'Food in Italy?' our friend said in despair. '*Pasta!*'

Pasta, with all its mad shapes, sums up the incredible diversity of Italian cooking: it is a staple of Italian gastronomic identity that can be shared by a whole nation and at the same time is adapted to every Italian individual's taste. There are hundreds of types of pasta and hundreds of thousands of pasta recipes. Every Italian who cooks has a unique recipe for meat sauce (ragù) (but they will all – and this is a profound Italian secret – let it simmer for *at least* a couple of hours).

Basically Italian cooking is idiosyncratic, even anarchic: in Italy 'home cooked' (in England a notoriously abused term) means just that – cooked in a particular way in that particular home by a particular person. In comparison, it is not so long ago that pasta in England meant tinned pasta – Heinz spaghetti in tomato sauce has

---

[23] In Italy, one of the authors of this book wishes to point out, everyone on early morning trains smells of fresh bread and roses. This may be a slightly biased view.

been around since 1926, and is still a major seller. Spaghetti Hoops date from the 1960s. And times change fairly slowly – back in 1992 the English cookery writer Nigel Slater (who is on record as saying that he is convinced that spaghetti is the Italians' idea of a practical joke) noted – in a possibly regrettable turn of phrase – that 'the British have finally embraced pasta.'

However, the reasons he gives might give most Italians pause: 'Its soft comforting form fits in with our love of bland, warming food, like porridge, bread sauce and rice pudding.' And, of course 'the best sauces will cook in the time it takes the pasta to cook.'(!)

But that's only fair: most Italians think that all the English eat is fish and chips, and roast beef; that everyone from Land's End to John o'Groats eats scrambled eggs and bacon for breakfast and that everyone stops whatever they are doing at 5pm to have tea.

PASTA – THE AWFUL TRUTH

(This is possibly the most SHOCKING revelation in this book!)

The Italians didn't invent pasta! It is true that the Romans used pasta layers and meat or sauce to make a kind of lasagne, but by then, in the Middle East they were already using thinner and longer dried pasta.

The first pasta factories were established in Sicily (where the Arab influence is stronger) in the twelfth century and from there they exported dried pasta to the South of Italy and to the rest of the Mediterranean, and then more factories were built around Italy.

National Obsessions

'When two Englishmen meet,' Dr Samuel Johnson said in the 18th century, 'their first talk is of the weather.'

The Italians have different preoccupations. As Beppe Severgnini points out in *La Bella Figura*: 'We talk about food before we eat it, while we're eating it, and after we've eaten it.' But, he goes on, there's more to it than that: 'It has been said that the digestive tract is a metaphysical entity in Italy, like lawns in England. This is true, but our obsession is more serious. The English don't eat their lawns.'

Italians take food very seriously – they like eating well, and they are knowledgeable about food: after all, they have bought their food in peasants' markets for centuries (and not for the past twenty years, as in England), and they don't grudge extra money if the quality is really good (frozen pre-cooked meals are not very common and until very recently they were even difficult to find in supermarkets). And this is true for Italians of all incomes – everybody is raised with the conviction that eating well is good for you, that you deserve it, and that really, saving money on food is a sin and a disgrace.

The English are rather the reverse: food, even in these expansive days, tends to be utilitarian. It's not that the English are food xenophobes – as we shall see, they have embraced world foods far more than the Italians: it is just that whatever the world food is – Thai, Chinese, Indian, Italian, it somehow becomes Anglicised (except in the most expensive restaurants!) – a form of fuel. As Nigel Slater wrote in *Eating for England*

> An ingredient from outer space has landed on the kitchen table. You know nothing about it other than the fact that it is edible... The Italians might grill it over charcoal and serve it up with olive oil and basil – that is, if they don't chuck it in with the fettuccine... What would the (English) do? *We would boil it.*

It's an attitude of mind that goes back a long way. Elizabeth David, in her pioneering book *Italian Food*, published in the rationing-ridden days of 1954 (and recently – ironically – blamed by

Antonio Carluccio for undervaluing native English cooking) started out by praising Italian cooks for the 'freshness and lavishness' of their raw materials. But the Italians were, she said, poorer than the English: the difference in what they did was an attitude of mind!

> When an Italian has not the wherewithal to cook one of the traditional extravagant dishes she doesn't attempt to produce an imitation. No amount of propaganda could persuade her to see the point of making a steak and kidney pudding with tinned beef and no kidneys... Her method would be to produce some attractive and nourishing little dish out of two ounces of cheese and a slice of ham, or a pound of spinach and a couple of eggs...

The best way to get someone from the North of Italy to become friendly with someone from the South is to talk about food (the equivalent in England has yet to be discovered).

And before we dip into history...

The contrast has never been summed up better than in the 1960 song with the inspired pairing of the eccentric English comic actor Peter Sellers and the quintessential Italian sex-symbol Sophia Loren. 'Bangers and Mash' a fantasy in which Sellers, as a British soldier, brings Loren 'back to Blighty just to show me mates.' But the result is, he hasn't 'had a decent meal since 1944': Loren urges Sellers to eat his minestrone, macaroni, tagliatelle and vermicelli, and Sellers replies 'Give us a bash at the bangers and mash me mother used to make!'

A MAGICAL HISTORY TOUR

or, When the English had to be Taught Table Manners

> *'Then must you learn the use and handling of your silver fork at meals'* (Sir Politic Would Be, in Ben Jonson's comedy *Volpone*, 1606).

The seriousness with which Italians approached cooking was considered eccentric even by the French as early as the 16th century.

Michel de Montaigne in his account of his journey to Italy (1581), describes a conversation with the steward of a famous Cardinal

> who replied with the science of guzzling, delivered with a magisterial gravity and demeanour as if he had been expounding some great point of theology. He spelled out to me the difference in appetites...the qualities of the ingredients and their effects; the differences in salads according to the season, which one should be warmed up and which served cold... And all this swollen with rich and magnificent words, and the way we use to talk about the government of an empire.

And this extended to table manners and eating implements. Thomas Coryat, a remarkable Englishman who walked from England to Venice in 1608, was impressed:

> I observed a custom in all those Italian cities and towns that I saw in my travels, neither do I think that any other nations of Christendom doth use it, but only Italy. The Italian and also most strangers that are commorant [resident] in Italy, doe always at their meals use a little fork when they cut their meat. (*He then explains just how this was done – we have left this out because these days most English readers probably know how.*) Whatsoever he be that fitting in the company of any others at meals, should unadvisedly touch the dish of meate with his fingers from which all at the table doe cut, he will give occasions of offence unto the company, as having transgressed the laws of good manners.

Poor Coryat was mocked in England for using a fork that he had brought back from Italy. Forks (made from silver or gold or even wood and tin) came to Italy in the 14th century and were commonly used by middle and upper classes by 1500 – most of Europe did not begin to use them until the 18th century: even at the sophisticated court of Louis XIV of France, they was not fully accepted.

Italian Renaissance Courts, even if they may have been considered cradles of political, religious, and sexual corruption, still provided the rest of Europe with courtly rules of polite behaviour and refinement. One of the most ancient handbooks of good manners, by Bonvesin de La Riva (1240-1314), a Latin teacher in Milan, includes the (obviously necessary) instructions

- do not talk with your mouth full
- do not talk about upsetting things when people are eating
- do not put elbows on the table[24]
- use napkins
- and do not 'disgust' your fellow diners by grabbing food from the table or stroking cats and dogs while eating ('disgust' is a recurrent word in his handbook).

Salad Days and Innovative Vegetables

Food historian Massimo Montanari thinks that the fork was first used in Italy because of pasta – it is easier to grab a leg of chicken with your hand than a mouthful of *pennette* with butter. But maybe the fork was invented to help to eat salad. Which (of course) the Italians also claim to have invented.

In the same year that Shakespeare made Cleopatra lament her salad days, Ben Jonson in his masque, *Hymenaei* compared the meaty English drama with the Italian style –

> a few Italian herbs, picked up and made into a sallad, may find sweeter acceptance than all the most nourishing and sound meats of the world.

Pietro Aretino (1492-1556) the Tuscan-born but Venice-based writer, who was a Renaissance hedonist and a good friend of Titian, recommends, in his letters, a salad of fresh mint leaves with plenty of

---

[24] By the way, the idea of eating from a fixed table in a special dining space, rather from a moveable table in a large communal hall, was introduced by Italian merchants. (Who else?)

chicory leaves, dressed with salt, vinegar and oil (which is the staple Italian dressing for salads nowadays and has been for time immemorial – the word 'salad' coming from the Latin 'salata' – salty).

The English have until very recently, had problems with salads, at least with dressing them. In G. K. Chesterton's 'The Salad of Colonel Cray' (1929) Father Brown, the modest detective, saves the life of the eponymous Colonel by mixing an emetic from the salad-cruet, which contains pepper, mustard, vinegar and oil. Clement Freud (grandson of Sigmund) thought that salads in England were generally naked and not oily because the 'clean cut English promoted utterly greaseless images.' And in any case, before the heady 1960s, olive oil was medicinal, and obtained from chemists' shops in small brown bottles.

The first *salad* cookery book was published (where else?) in Italy as early as 1570, written by a botanist and doctor, Costanzo Felici da Piobbico (in the Marche region): *Lettera sopra l'insalata e piante che in qualunque modo vengono per cibo del'homo* (*A Letter upon Salad and Plants that can be Food for Man*). It discusses hundreds of kinds of herbs and lettuce that one can find in fields or cultivate in orchards – but he also admits that it is only the Italians who like salads and vegetables – and they are often mocked by foreigners who think that eating raw herbs and salads means 'togliere la vivanda agli animali bruti' (depriving brute animals of their food).

POPE DIES OF HAM DEFICIENCY

Dateline 1471: Pope Paul II has died of melon indigestion, after ignoring the advice of the medical profession that the 'hot' of the ham was the perfect counterbalance for the 'cold' of the fruit. 'At least, that's our story,' said a Vatican spokesperson.

It wasn't only pasta and salads that Italy gave to the European diet: it was vegetables, too. Italians believed that there was much that the poor could teach the rich in culinary matters, and vegetables became important in the national diet. Artichokes were almost certainly bred (from the thistle) by Italian horticulturists in the 15th century; eating peas was a fashion that came from Italy in the Middle Ages.

Potatoes weren't quite so lucky – they have never been as central to the Italian diet as to the English. They were treated with suspicion for centuries, and it wasn't until the 1700s that peasants were finally convinced to accept this 'white truffle', as it was called, as food and as a crop to seriously cultivate.

When Pellegrino Artusi wrote his *La scienza in cucina* (1891) for the rising middle classes only thirty years after the political unification of Italy, he introduced several recipes with potatoes, but when he described the recipe for potato salad he still felt the need to justify their use: 'Although we are talking about potatoes', he writes, 'I can tell you that this dish, in its modesty, deserves to be praised.' *Although we are talking about potatoes!*

Mind you, he was not alone: Mrs Beeton, in her *Book of Household Management* (1861) noted: 'The whole of the family are suspicious; a great number are narcotic, and many are deleterious.' She then gives twelve recipes for them!

The Literature of Cookery

Naturally enough, all this variety and innovation was reflected in Italian cookery books. The most famous cook of the Renaissance, Bartolomeo Scappi (1500-1577), who ended his career as the Pope's cook, writes in his volume of 1000 recipes that he learned how to cook turbot from the fishermen of Chioggia and Venice: 'li quali fanno i migliori pottaggi, che in tutti i liti del mare' ('who make the best fish soup of all the seaside places').

In 1548, Ortensio Lando, from Milan, imagined a gastronomic tour of Italy, from the Alps to Sicily, illustrating local specialities – especially sausages and salami (cured meats, then as now, were, with olives, and pickles, very important as *Antipasto Italiano*). Maestro Martino, the most famous Italian cook of the 15th century, devotes a whole chapter of his recipe book *Libro de Arte Coquinaria*, to *frittelle* – that infinitely varied species of fried dough goodies of which there are perhaps only three or four varieties in England. (In the 17th century, English donuts looked very much like *frittelle*.)

Many cookery books emphasised regional differences, but the nationalising of Italian cuisine for the new nation came with Pellegrino Artusi's *Scienza in Cucina e l'Arte di Mangiar Bene* (1891), which collects all regional variations of recipes and offers them to the middle classes of united Italy as *Italian cooking*. His book became *the* Italian cookery book (the book given to newly married women, for example) for many decades and it is believed that it did more to instil a notion of Italian identity than many political strategies. Its secret lay in the fact that it did not attempt to erase regional variations – food diversity was accepted as an inescapable fact of Italian identity. This can be seen, for example, when Artusi discusses frying:

> Ogni popolo usa per friggere quell'unto che si produce migliore nel proprio paese. In Toscana si dà la preferenza all'olio, in Lombardia al burro e nell'Emilia al lardo che vi si prepara eccellente. (All people use the fat that is the best produce of that area for frying. In Tuscany they prefer oil, in Lombardy, butter, and in Emilia they use lard, which they produce in an excellent way.)

Artusi's cookery book increased in size every year with the feedback (as it were) of readers, from the 475 initial recipes to the 790 of the final edition. It is still in print and it has been one of the best-selling books in Italy.

English cookery books, on the other hand, tended to celebrate the largesse of a nation that in the 18th and 19th centuries fed itself well (always excepting the peasantry). Two of the most famous, Hannah Glasse's *The Art of Cookery* (1747) and Eliza Acton's *Modern*

Cookery for Private Families (1845) included staggeringly rich recipes with vast quantities of eggs and cream. The 1868 edition includes 'A Neapolitan Receipt' for 'Stufato', which consists of boiling six pounds of silver side of beef, herbs and four pounds of butter for six hours, then adding three pounds of macaroni boiled for twenty-five minutes and half a pint of 'very pure salad oil' – and, just in case we're getting too exotic – half a small clove of garlic; 'before serving up, sprinkle Parmesan cheese thickly on the maccaroni.' She concludes:

> We insert this receipt exactly as it was given to us by a friend, at whose table the dish was served with great success to some Italian diplomatists. From our own slight experience of it, we must observe that three pounds would make too gigantic a dish to enter well, on ordinary occasions, into an English service.

Acton's successor and plagiarist, Mrs Beeton (who was not only deeply suspicious of potatoes, but also disliked garlic, lobsters, mangoes and cheese) developed the noble English tradition of publishing foreign recipes which never existed in their native countries. The section on Italian cooking in a 1950s edition of *Mrs Beeton's Family Cookery* includes: Maccharoni al latte (macaroni with cheese); Gallinaccio alla Milanese (turkey, chestnuts, prunes and pears); Choux de Bruxelles al Simone (*sic* – although she undoubtedly meant limone) and Lódola con cipolla (stuffed larks with onion).

In the UK, according to *The Bookseller*, cookery books account for about 10% of the physical book market, and while book sales overall are declining rapidly, cookery books have increased their sales by five times over the past five years. But these are not day to day, utilitarian books – these are kitchen fantasies.

Fantasies, food and fiction...

Food fantasies go back a long way.

Exquisite meals at Renaissance courts were in stark contrast to the everyday diet of the Italian peasant who dreamed of filling his stomach. In Boccaccio's *Decameron* (1348) we find a version of the Land of Cockaygne, here called Bengodi ('enjoy well'), the fantasy of a place or a space with enormous amounts of food and drink, and where restrictions and aestheticism are reversed and parodied:

> The district is called Bengodi, and there they bind the vines with sausages, and a denier will buy a goose and a gosling into the bargain; and on a mountain, all of grated Parmesan cheese, dwell folk that do nought else but make macaroni and raviuoli, and boil them in capon's broth, and then throw them down to be scrambled for; and hard by flows a rivulet of Vernaccia, the best that ever was drunk, and never a drop of water therein.... Were it nigher, I warrant thee, I would go with thee thither one while, just to see the macaroni come tumbling down, and take my fill thereof.

We know now that these macaroni of the Middle Ages, were, in fact, *gnocchi* – before the potato was introduced in Europe gnocchi in Italy were made of flour, egg, breadcrumbs, and cheese – similar to the knödel that in the Alpine regions are still so popular nowadays. Potato gnocchi is the result of the encounter of a product from the New World – the potato, and an Old World cooking practice. A parallel example is chips in England: they represent the encounter of potatoes and oil which was unknown in the Americas.

There is plenty of food in English Literature, although the English are, naturally, a little suspicious of it – and it tends to gravitate to children's books, where adult readers can indulge fantasies of comfort-eating. The Rat's picnic basket in *The Wind in the Willows* (1908), that most regressive of pre-First World War fantasies, famously contained

'Coldtonguecoldhamcoldbeefpickledgherkinssaladfrenchrollscr esssandwidgespottedmeatgingerbeerlemonadesodawater...'

Enid Blyton's 'Famous Five' novels contained food orgies that must have been highly satisfying in food-deprived post-war England. Here is a 'high tea' from *Five Go Down to the Sea* (1954):

There was an enormous tureen of new potatoes, all gleaming with melted butter, scattered with parsley. There was a big bottle of home-made salad cream. 'And look at the cream cheese, too' marvelled Dick, quite overcome. 'And that fruit cake. And are those drop-scones... and there's a cherry tart and cream...'

Not everyone enjoyed this self-indulgence: Evelyn Waugh's *Brideshead Revisited* (1945) was criticised at the time for 'glorying in gastronomic excess'!

The Language of Life

Identifying people with their food is an ancient practice (as when the ancient Greeks defined themselves as bread-eaters to distinguish themselves from the Barbarians, who were hunters). When Garibaldi took over the South of Italy on behalf of the North in 1860 and Naples was annexed to Piedmont, Prime Minister Cavour wrote to the Piedmontese ambassador to Paris referring to Garibaldi's take-over in culinary terms: 'The Macaroni is ready, and we will eat it.' Italians who emigrated at the beginning of the 20th century were called Macaronis, the typical dish of Naples and most of the South of Italy. (And in the American folksong, 'Yankee Doodle', the feather stuck in the cap refers to the foppish Englishmen of the Macaroni club, who had acquired their dandyish fashions from the Grand Tour – which, of course, included Italy.)[25]

And times don't change.

Not long ago, there were political demonstrations in the Veneto. A demonstrator wearing the green scarf of the Lega party was waving a placard reading 'SI alla polenta, NO al couscous' ('Yes to polenta, no to couscous'). Next to him, a middle-aged man of African origin waved a placard reading 'Piu couscous meno polenta' ('More couscous, less polenta').

---

[25] English macaroon biscuits get their name from maccaroni, via the French macaron. They were first baked in Venice in the 14th century.

It would seem that food and Italy are one: food and England are still a little, or a trifle, conflicted...

So now we can venture out to see what each country has to offer us, food-wise.

Chapter 9

Eating (and Drinking) Out and In

Prologue –

A DREAM OF FAIR EATING

Somewhere in a parallel universe, where things have gone right, there is a little village on Planet Foodie, where Italy and England meet – let's call it Little Santo Stefano in-the-Wold. In the middle of the village is an open space … and a red dividing line. On the English side, where there are fluffy clouds in the sky, it seems to be a village green, with grass and a duck pond and a wooden bench and behind that are low thatched cottages, with white walls and black beams; on the Italian side, where it's rather more sunny and dusty, it's a piazza, with a fountain, and worn paving stones and tall houses with balconies, terra-cotta tile roofs, and tables with sun umbrellas.

It looks like a place – and it is – where you can find the best food in two countries – so come for a stroll with us, and bring your appetite! (And we're not talking about the high end, here – this is not coffee at Florian's in St Mark's Square in Venice (E8 a cup), or High Tea at the Ritz in London (£125 for two) – this is real life.)

In the morning, the best place to be is on the Italian side, where there is a tiny corner shop, with large glass windows. It's bright and deep and narrow, with a gleaming bar along one side, where the customers are leaning and drinking miniature cups of espresso. There are display cases with rows of gorgeously designed tiny cakes and piles of tiny croissants – just a mouthful, because this is not a place where you stay. Nobody is in a hurry (except the virtuosa on the coffee machine – who can serve twenty cups while her English counterpart would still be finding the saucers – Italians take coffee *very* seriously), and everyone is very friendly, but they don't stay long. If you want a longer chat, cross the red line again and stroll across the square to the English Tea-Room, with its low beams, polished wooden tables, large cups, and substantial buns. (But don't drink the coffee.)

And for lunch... There's the smart English gastro pub – low beams, local draft beers (neither fizzy nor particularly cold) and large plates with seared scallops or slow-cooked belly pork – and elegantly served chips. Or we could go across the green/square and sit on a high stool in the Venetian *cicchetti* bar, with its piles of savoury rolls, or white sandwiches (*tramezzini*) neatly bulging with delicacies such as tuna mayo with silverskin onions or asparagus and halved boiled eggs or piles of shaved ham and cheese and capers and artichokes .... washed down with a very acceptable glass of red of wine from the pump on the bar – in Venice such a glass is called *un'ombra* (a shadow).

We can then while away the afternoon sitting on the wooden bench, watching the cricket match, with a couple of pints of local beer (and packets of crisps – which we paid for), and feeding the ducks; or we can kick back under the sun-umbrellas with a *mezzo litro* (half a litre) of local wine (and *free* crisps[26] and sometimes free mini-pastries and savouries) and feed the pigeons.

---

[26] We have heard it seriously argued that the ubiquitous free crisps alone demonstrate the superiority of Italian over English culture (never mind Michelangelo and the rest).

And in the evening, when the cultural gastronomic gulf widens... First there are two magnificent English institutions, and in Little Santo Stefano they are sublime examples of their type (there are, of course, tens of thousands of very un-sublime examples elsewhere.) But the fish and chip shop, which, much like the *cicchetti* bar, hasn't really changed since Formica became fashionable in the 1950s, sells us hot crisp golden batter with chunks of steaming white fish inside, and ... chips. And salt and malt vinegar. Aficionados may pass through to the Spartan interior and eat skate wings with black butter and capers... but that's about as exotic as the chip shop gets.   For the exotic, we go next door, to the Indian restaurant – with its obligatory flock wallpaper – where charming staff serve highly eclectic and highly spiced foods, some of which are actually authentically Indian – and we drink cold Indian lager (brewed in Burton-upon-Trent).

But if neither of these places exist in Italy, we cross the line again, and what awaits us across the square is something that doesn't exist in England. First we go into a modest restaurant: it has nothing to distinguish it, in fact it's rather scruffy (although scrupulously clean). There are wine racks, and the menu is worn and not particularly inventive or informative. The staff are local, the clientele range from the well-heeled to the council rubbish-collectors.   But the next thing we notice is that the house wine costs only 10% more than you would pay in a supermarket – and then that the food comes quickly, and is simple, beautifully cooked, top quality – and – like it or not – HUGE portions. There is crisp pizza, mounds of creamy gnocchi, a jumble of fried squid and prawns (with a segment of lemon as a gesture towards vegetables). Now the point about this place for the English is not that it's excellent, or cheap, or classless – but that you can find somewhere like it anywhere in Italy.

And the other place to eat in the evening (or all day, come to that) that you don't find in England isn't in the square at all[27].

So we have to leave the idyllic square and walk a few hundred yards, or metres, towards the petrol station and the newish housing estate. It is neat and well-kept, but not particularly prosperous and certainly not quaint. If this were England, there might just be a corner shop, but nothing else.

This being Italy, there is a corner shop, but let us turn down this quiet residential street for another five minutes' walk, and, among the houses is a house with slightly bigger windows and a discreet sign. Walk in, and you're in a neat and tidy neighbourhood restaurant, almost certainly family-run. Here you will get excellent home-made pasta, veal, or roast guinea fowl, or local specialities. It will be relatively cheap, clean and friendly. Amazing.

Then, maybe, to end the evening, we might cross the line again and sit in the chimney-corner of our pub, by a log fire in the winter (and a lot of the summer) and have a nightcap of coffee laced with whisky and cream ...

But, back in the real world, what do we need to know before venturing out for a coffee, or a take-away, or to a restaurant, or into someone's home to eat?

---

[27] At this point, the authors would like to admit to a division of opinion. Laura finds the next place that we are about to visit so ordinary that it's not really worth mentioning. Peter finds it so extraordinary that it's worth the walk. Or even the air fare.

DRINKING COFFEE or how a bar works in Italy

Before we venture into one of the hundreds of thousands of small bars you can find in every town and every village in Italy – some lean towards cakes and coffee, some towards alcohol and snacks – a word on the philosophy of these places. They are not places for sitting down and being waited on: Italians drink and snack – graze – and move on.

And so treating someone to a coffee in Italy is not the time-consuming thing it might be in England. It can be a non-committal way of making friends with people you don't know well, or even of *deciding* whether you want to make friends at all. 'Ti offro un caffè?' ('Shall I treat you to a coffee?') implies something innocent and quick – you never say no, unless you have a pressing engagement and you are really late. You get to drink your coffee, make conversation for three or four minutes and then you are left with the time to decide whether you want to see that person again for another coffee, or perhaps for lunch or dinner. Lots of friendships start with the innocent 'ti offro un caffé'. Or even relationships. Think of it, among other things, as a cheap form of speed dating!

There's not really a word for these places in English, but whatever we call them, there are no *chains* of these 'bars' in Italy – no Caffè Nero or Costa or Prêt à Manger or EAT or Bagel Factory or Delice de France or Upper Crust. Every bar is different and individual, with its individual (and often eccentric) regulars. But they have one thing in common. FAST service – and often FURIOUS as one or two people will have to make coffee simultaneously for eight customers who need to order, drink their coffee standing up and pay in the space of three minutes. That is why cappuccinos MUST not be served hot and in a mug, as they need to be gulped down in exactly the same time as an espresso and why Italian barmen or barwomen need to be able to multitask if they want to survive!) It is a fascinating experience to see a regular customer entering a bar and lifting his finger to indicate 'ONE coffee' (you don't have to add 'please' when you are ordering at a bar – they won't expect it) and by the time he gets to the counter, his coffee will be ready. (If you order 'un caffé' you will be served an espresso of course.)

Just try the same thing at King's Cross station at 8.00 pm. There are only four customers and they are in a slow queue. By the time you get to the counter it's already 8.15 pm. Then you place your order with someone. You pay. Then they pass your order to someone else who proceeds to make coffee. Then they give you a bucketful that you will drink on the train (in Italy they don't generally do takeaway coffee – no need to!).

ITALIAN'S BID TO SOLVE CULTURAL COFFEE CLASH THWARTED

Salvo Montegrotto's (29) attempt to become a millionaire by selling Italian-sized coffee cups with extra long handles outside Starbucks, Costa, and other English coffee-house chains has failed after a series of mysterious accidents. Signor Montegrotto's idea was that six customers could buy one set of his coffee cups, and then purchase one cup of coffee in the coffee-house and share it between them by dipping. 'It's amazing how clumsy people are outside coffee-houses,' Signor Montegrotto said from his hospital bed in London: 'they kept on bumping into me and breaking my cups.' His previous campaign to encourage drinkers to refuse to pay for their crisps was also unsuccessful.

In recent years, English coffee drinkers have become used to espresso (or expresso!) and cappuccino and mocha and an increasing range of exotic brews – some, like Gingerbread Latte Flat White which are impossible to find in Italy. Italy has far more that are difficult to find in England – for example, the Italians distinguish between macchiato *caldo* (with hot milk) and macchiato *freddo* (with cold milk in a separate mini jug), then there is *macchiatone* (something between macchiato and cappuccino), *corretto* (with grappa or other liqueurs), *shakerato* (shaken with crushed ice and sugar), and *schiumato* (with just a little milk foam). And – of course –

there are regional variations as well. For example, in Trieste if you want an espresso you have to order 'un nero', if you want a cappuccino 'un capo' and so on.

But remember – don't ever order a 'latte'. Latte, in Italian, means just 'milk' – so you will be given a glass of that. The closest to English 'latte' is Italian 'latte macchiato'.

They Do Things Differently There

The Alert English Reader might have noticed something odd, or un-English about that account: the bit that read 'customers who need to order, drink their coffee standing-up and pay' – because it happens in that order. There's an ancient English joke (class-based, of course) in which a young lady returns from a first date and reports: 'It was very posh! We paid *after* we ate!' In England, the procedure for anything in the rapid-food line is order, pay, collect, which does seem slightly more logical: in the admittedly magical Italian coffee bar, you have to queue twice, once to be served and once again to tell the cashier what you just had: it's a wonderfully trusting system.

However, when you get to the Italian version of what in England would be called a snack bar – whether on the street or at an airport or station or motorway service area – the reverse system applies. You inspect the food on display, decide what you want, tell a cashier (who may be quite a long way from the food, so you can't point at it), and pay. You then take your receipt back to the counter and collect your food. As you can see, this is not a system designed for the linguistically challenged.

How Pizza Conquered England, and Italy Repulsed the Curry Invasion – and the Strange Case of the Italian Meatball

Here is a revealing statistic: the largest fast-food company in the world, Subway, has around 40,000 'outlets' worldwide: in 2013, the UK had 1,544 of them. And Italy had... 17. The second largest,

McDonalds, has over 1200 restaurants in the UK, and just over 400 in Italy (where you might get a 'Gran Crispy McBacon Edizione Limitata').

Long gone are the 1950s, when pizza was marketed in England as 'Welsh Rarebit Pie', and the first pizza restaurant in London rapidly went out of business. Pizza has swept the world, and retail chains such as Pizza Hut, Pizza Express and Domino's Pizza supply a huge English appetite for them. In contrast, pizza chains hardly exist in Italy.

And as for curry houses: in the UK in 2013 there were an estimated 10,000 Indian restaurants turning over (as it were) £3.2 *billion*. Chicken tikka masala (invented in Glasgow) has become a national dish – overtaking, by some reports, fish and chips – although the number of fish and chip shops is still slightly greater – about 10,500 nationwide. Incidentally, it is claimed that the spread of fish and chips through the British Isles in the nineteenth century was due to Italian entrepreneurs. If you want fish and chips in Dublin, you ask for 'one and one' – which is an echo of the first fish-and-chip seller in Ireland – Giuseppe Cervi, whose wife would ask the customers 'Uno di questa, uno di quella?' ('One of this, one of that?'). But you would be hard pressed to find a fish and chip shop in Italy, and curry houses are rare: Tripadvisor lists 4,900 restaurants in Milan – of which only 35 are Indian.

And so there is a profound paradox about eating out in Italy and England. The English used to be considered a deeply conservative gastronomic nation – but they have, literally, gobbled up cuisines from around the world. The Italians, with their spectacular variety of native dishes, generally eat only Italian food.

One entertaining result of this English eclecticism is that restaurants outside Italy commonly serve 'Italian' dishes unheard of in Italy. The most famous (or notorious) of these is *spaghetti meatballs*, a dish created by the Italian immigrants in the USA. In the 2014 Italian edition of *Masterchef*, the contestants had to prepare this dish in honour of Joe Bastianich, the American judge of Italian origin. The look of horror and surprise and general disapproval (and sense of superiority) of the contestants was really something as they watched

Joe, in his very approximate Italian, explain to them how to make it – and then expect them to prepare it the same way as his mother. Needless to say, most contestants failed miserably.

Indeed, the dish became iconic, with the song 'One Meat Ball (and no Spaghetti)' – a Second World War hit – and the romantic scene in Walt Disney's *Lady and the Tramp* (1955) when Tramp takes Lady to Tony's Italian restaurant where they have 'Two spaghetti a-speciale, heavy on the-a meat-a-balls.'

Another dish that you will never see on a menu in Italy is *Macaroni Cheese*. You won't find *Eggs Florentine* or *Garibaldi biscuits* either. As for *Spaghetti Bolognese*, you may just find it but if you do, it means that you are eating in a VERY touristy place (your chance to RUN!). If you find on your Italian menu something called *Zuppa Inglese*, this is not English soup: we have found it translated in an English cookery book as 'trifle Italian-style.'

We could fill this book with such oddities, such as 'Salad of Trevise with Pickled Walnuts,' or 'Crab mac-n-cheese,' but the English are not unique in naturalising food: in some Chinese restaurants in Italy noodle dishes are made with spaghetti!

And of course, Italy not being a particularly horse-loving country, eating horses is OK in many areas, so horsemeat can be found in several shapes and sizes: from grilled steaks to meat sauce, from carpaccio to tartare, from stew to *horse*burgers – and on pizzas.

And in the Restaurants…

HEALTH HAZARD IN ENGLISH RESTAURANTS

Last week the English Health and Safety Executive closed down three restaurants, when a surprise inspection revealed children on the premises. 'We were shocked,' said Chief Inspector Arthur Grunt. 'In two cases, the child was actually IN THE DINING AREA when a meal was being served. This is totally unhygienic and would cause acute emotional distress to diners. Where do these people think they are? Italy?'

Yes: in Italy you will find *children* in restaurants in the evenings; this is perfectly acceptable – especially in the summer when they don't have to get up early the next morning to go to school (most of Italian schoolchildren's holidays are concentrated in one big three-month period in the summer – they get only three days off at Easter and less than two weeks at Christmas). So if you see parents having a good time at a restaurant and children having an even better time at 11.00 pm (in Italy a good time to start eating is between 8.00 pm and 9.00 pm – possibly earlier in the North, and later in the South) don't call the emergency Childline, or even its Italian equivalent, the *telefono azzurro* (blue phone). It's OK.

Once the English have recovered from the shock of such activity at knee-height, they encounter an oddity of the Italian menu.

Unlike the French and the English, who have a main course, 'framed' by a starter and dessert, the traditional Italian meal consists of a starter – antipasto – then TWO main courses (and – if you wish – dessert as well). The first course (*il primo*) would be a dish of pasta or rice or soup and a second course (*il secondo*), meat or fish. This can be confusing to the English, and nowadays Italians don't always have two main courses when they eat at home – and they often choose only one main dish when they order in a restaurant. It's useful to know that you can order one course at a time: the English, used to ordering starter and main course together, often find themselves overfaced by the generous portions of the antipasto, let alone the *primo piatto*.

117

So, where does this tradition to have two courses come from? Massimo Montanari believes that in the Middle Ages, when meat was easily available in Italy, the meal structure was the same as in the other European countries. But slowly meat became more expensive and therefore less and less common until it disappeared from the diet of the peasants and the lower classes. As Montaigne observed while he was travelling in Italy in the 16th century, 'this nation is not in the habit of eating much meat' – the Italian diet being based more on grains and vegetables. At the end of the 19th century, Italy was a poor country. The average consumption of meat was 16 kilos per person per annum (in Germany, it was 40 kilos, in Britain, 58 kilos). Pasta, which until then had been just a side dish for meat (as it still is in France, for example) became a main dish. So pasta and meat exchanged places: meat became a side dish for pasta, in the form of meat sauce (ragù). The same happened in the regions where rice or polenta were more common than pasta.

In the 20th century, meat became affordable again and returned to Italian tables but the habit of having a pasta or rice-based main dish was entrenched. Pasta didn't disappear but was served separately from the meat main course. The structure of the menu doubled, and there were two protagonists. There still are! Pasta, after all, is a cultural necessity: 'What is the glory of Dante compared with spaghetti?' the Italian writer Giuseppe Prezzolini wondered in 1954. But spaghetti and pizza *are* a part of Italian civilization as much as Dante and Petrarch and Fellini, and they are part of a legacy that has spread throughout the world. As food historians Capatti and Montanari have observed: 'without realizing it, when we eat spaghetti, we also ingest something of Dante.'

And there is one other obvious difference between Italian restaurants in Italy and Italian restaurants outside Italy: in Italy the structure of the dish is different – food is not piled on the plate – there is no concept of 'on a bed of'. Italian plates come with the main ingredient – meat or pasta or fish – and very often you will have to order vegetables separately. Italians just don't pile food on plates, however artistically!

WINE LEAGUE TABLES SHOCK HORROR!
ITALY COMES 1st *AND* 9th IN PER CAPITA DRINKING!

'This in unfair,' said the President of the English Binge Drinkers Association. 'They have two slurps of the bottle.' The President of the Italian Wine Society responded: 'This is a characteristic misunderstanding by the drunken English; the Vatican City, which takes first place and is unbeatable for its consumption, is not part of Italy.'

The English have for years, in their modest and rather gloomy way, assumed that everyone in Europe drinks more than they do – the Italians they regard as cheerful, carefree, sunshine drinkers. Italy has a warm, partying feel about it, so naturally the Italians must drink vast quantities of Cinzano and Campari, Prosecco and Chianti, and are generally the happier for it.

Surprisingly, the statistics seem to bear most of this out. Given that Italian beer has never been particularly distinguished (although Peroni and Nastro Azzurro are among SABMiller's big brands) and the image of cakes and ale well-established in the English persona, the fact that the UK is 19th in per capita beer consumption and Italy 41st, comes as no surprise. Nor do the league table positions for wine-drinking – Italy 9th, UK, 39th – although things are much closer when it comes to overall consumption – Italy third, UK fifth.

But the thing is – if you visit Italy, you would never know that Italians drink a lot, because Italians drink differently. It is not simply that over the past thirty years there has been a steady decrease in wine drinking, rather that wine has always been considered something for everyday consumption, in moderation. It is part of growing up in families: teenagers are invited to taste a little wine with water – but, most importantly, wine is commonly drunk with meals and the idea that it must complement the food is a very strong one.

True, Italians drink at different times from the English – the sight of Venetians enjoying their post-breakfast spritz (a mixture of Prosecco, Aperol and water)[28], or elderly ladies or gentlemen having a mid-morning glass of wine at a bar – is a little disconcerting. It is also counter-intuitive that the North of Italy drinks more than the South and the hard-working Northeast – the Veneto – the most.

But the simple fact is that on social occasions Italians generally do not drink very much at all. A group of Italians sitting around a sunny restaurant table will take a long time to get to a second round of drinks. And many English guests at dinner in a restaurant, or in an Italian home must have been surprised, if not actually traumatised, by the behaviour of their hosts regarding drinks. Italians, it can hardly be emphasised enough – are possibly the most spontaneously generous people on earth – but put a bottle of wine on the table in front of them, and to the English mind, something strange happens. In fact, after the first glass or two *nothing* seems to happen. In England (assuming we are not in the servant-zone) the host will assiduously, often too assiduously, keep wine-glasses topped up. In Italy, the wine bottle will sit, unmolested, on the table. Occasionally, a guest or family member will refresh his own glass, but even the guest whose glass has tactically been emptied at the same rate as his hosts' will not be offered more. Last year, at a very convivial evening party in a restaurant in Naples, we watched a hapless Englishman with an empty glass stare in mute horror as his host ordered a new bottle and poured himself a small glass from it – and the bottle then remained untouched until the party left.

And so here is a vital piece of advice, which goes against the very core of English behaviour: help yourself! The Italian host would not presume to judge how much wine his guests should have: they can decide for themselves!

---

[28] Spritz originated in Austria and there are a good many variants – a spritz can contain Select or Campari instead of Aperol, and in Trieste spritz is made with soda and wine (by the way, the new five boy band from Trieste calls itself 'Spritz for Five'!). The English 'spritzer' is usually just wine and fizzy water, so you confuse them at your peril!

Italy is a nation, then, which has a mature and generally balanced relationship to alcohol – although times are changing. This is what Mussolini wrote about wine in 1933:

> the problem of alcoholism, the way they have it in the Northern countries, does not exist in Italy. Italians drink exclusively wine. And wine is a product of Western civilization; the delicious product of vineyards and grapes of the Mediterranean, born from the joyful marriage of the sun, the sky and the earth. Whoever speaks of wine, therefore, speaks of the civilization of the white human race.

Leaving aside the unpleasant racist touch at the end, Mussolini's image of Italians and their wine consumption, this has always been only partly true. Recently there has been a shift to weekend drinking, with an emphasis – as in England – on beer and spirits. Even now, though, Italian young people tend to drink less than their counterparts elsewhere in Europe, although the Erasmus Generation is helping to change things!

The Three Great Virtues

Just in case we had missed anything, we asked an Italophile English friend of ours for the top three differences between eating and drinking in Italy and in England. He put down his pint, and said, 'You mean, apart from quantity.' We nodded: after all, it goes without saying that English food and drink are generally judged by quantity – which is why top class restaurants stand out by serving small portions. 'Easy,' our friend said:

1. Friendliness
2. Cleanliness of the loos
and
3. You always get a little spoon to pick up the peanuts with.

Which sums it all up very nicely.

But our friend forgot to mention the roses. Rose-sellers haunt Italian restaurants – sometimes, perhaps, not with the desired effect.

A couple of years ago, some English and Italian friends were walking home from a restaurant across the market in Turin, when a young woman in her twenties (with a couple of female friends) came bouncing down the street towards them carrying a huge bunch of red roses and handing them out merrily to any passer-by. The English naturally tried to pretend that she was invisible and that something so unseemly wasn't happening; the Italians naturally wanted to know what was going on. It turned out that the woman's boyfriend had been horrible to her, so she had dumped him; he had then returned contritely with the huge bunch of roses, which she had accepted, and then promptly dumped him again. She was now giving them away to everyone: gestures speak louder than words.

This could only happen in Italy…

Chapter 10

Viva la Differenza!

So – a world of amazing differences – but how to sum them up?

Perhaps we could compare Dante with Shakespeare, Thomas Cromwell with Machiavelli, Garibaldi with Henry V – or even Stella McCartney with Donatella Versace?

Or are there things even more quintessentially English or Italian?

The English Tourist Board – that genial purveyor of sunlit fantasy – is inclined to offer Morris Dancing as the ultimate image of Englishness. The dancers have colourful costumes with bells and ribbons on their legs, wave sticks and swords and handkerchiefs – and the dances go back to the fifteenth century. There are many very local variants – and they are commonly greeted with a mixture of delight and amusement. But Italy is no slouch (*non è da meno*) when it comes to local folk dancing – and the variations are as rich and colourful as local food: the Lachera dancers of the Piedmont would (and possibly do) feel at home with the Morrismen of the Cotswolds.

So, for a comparison, we could try looking at music.

Opera vs The Ukes

Italy is the seat – and the great exporter – of great opera, with all its colour and drama and extrovert extravagance – things that are quintessentially Italian. And England...

Let us rush – gallop – to insist that when it comes to opera, England has world-class singers and word-class companies: the English National Opera can stand beside any company from anywhere. It is innovative and eclectic – and yet, when we look at its 2013-14 programme, what do we find? The operas for adults include one by Bizet, one by Tchaikovsky and one by Wagner. There is *Sweeney Todd* (by an American). And *The Marriage of Figaro* (originally with an Italian libretto, of course) *Girl of the Golden West, La Boheme, Orpheo,* and *La Traviata.* And an opera by Purcell (who incorporated Italian influences into his work). A certain dominance there, would you say? (This, it must be said, is almost exactly the same proportion of Italian operas to operas from other countries that appear on the programme for the Teatro Alla Scala, Milano, 2014.)

But if opera means Italy, what music expresses the essence of England?

How about the eight Ukuleles of The Ukulele Orchestra of Great Britain? The ukulele in England was popularised in the 1930s and 1940s by singer George Formby. In the hands of the virtuoso eight-person 'Ukulele Orchestra', its reputation has been transformed. The 'Ukes', immaculate in formal evening dress, have travelled the concert halls of the world to rave reviews, exploiting their English eccentricity through the incongruity of small, cheap instruments playing every style of music. Perhaps most spectacularly, they played an arrangement of 'Ode to Joy' for 1000 Ukuleles during the 2012 BBC Promenade Concerts at the Royal Albert Hall, and have a remarkable version of 'Danse Macabre' for eight ukuleles.

Pavarotti, versus eight ukuleles: now *that* makes a contrast.

Or film…

Sophia Loren versus Margaret Rutherford

'Everything you see, I owe to spaghetti' – *attributed to Sophia Loren.*

'The unique thing about Margaret Rutherford is that she can act with her chin alone.' – *Kenneth Tynan*

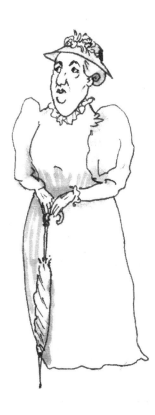

After the Second World War, both countries set about rebuilding their film industries: Italy had the advantage of the revitalised fascist-built Cinecittà in Rome, and England the disadvantage of the quota battle with Hollywood – but what they produced says a lot about the countries' psyches.

The picture, as it were, is complicated, but in the 1940s and 1950s, Italy produced a series of existential masterpieces, whose directors have internationally-recognised names – Rossellini's, *Roma Città Aperta* (1945), De Sica's *Ladri di Biciclette* (1948) and *Umberto D* (1952), Fellini's *La Strada* (1954) and *La Dolce Vita* (1960). (These apart from sunny American co-productions such as *Roman Holiday* (1953) for which Audrey Hepburn won an Oscar.)

In England there were occasional *noirs* such as Carol Reed's *The Third Man* (1947), but the staples were comedies with varying degrees of bite such as *The Ladykillers* (1955) and *The Lavender Hill Mob* (1951) and patriotic-stiff-upper-lip war films such as *The Dam Busters* (1952) and *The Cruel Sea* (1952). A different dynamic, but curiously reflecting national characteristics: England in nostalgic retreat, Italy in agonised recovery.

The contrast might be better summed up by the leading men and women. Marcello Mastroianni, the suave, tall, handsome, perhaps louche and subtly corrupt leading man, epitomised for the world all of Italy (and Italian men) in *La Dolce Vita* – about corrupt high society. In contrast, in England, the quintessential English male was represented by the short, genial Kenneth More, so good at wittily confronting the Germans as the flying ace Douglas Bader in *Reach for the Sky* (1956) or helping to sink the Bismarck, or playing the cad in the comedy celebrating the London to Brighton vintage car race, *Genevieve* (Cornelius, 1953).

Even more illuminating is the contrast between Sophia Loren and pretty well any English actress of the period. Through the 1950s, Loren developed into an international sex-symbol, often acting with Marcello Mastroianni; in England her only equivalent was Diana Dors, who, despite being an intelligent and not inconsiderable actress, made the prudish English rather uncomfortable. Much more characteristic of the English idea of the acceptable and unthreatening female was Margaret Rutherford. From Madame Arcati in Noël Coward's *Blithe Spirit* (Lean, 1945) to her series of films in the 1960s as the definitive Miss Marple, Agatha Christie's spinster detective, Rutherford encapsulated a deceptive combination of apparent comfortableness and innocence and high (and sometimes threatening) intelligence. She had as many curves as Loren, but not in the same places.

Or we might compare detectives...

Lewis versus Montalbano

In deepest England, a Northerner not much interested in the North, the dour Detective Inspector Robbie Lewis explores intellectual murders, against the backdrop of a picturesque and civilised Oxford. He slowly forgets about his dead wife, and edges his way towards a calm and restrained relationship with his Laura. He has a quietly witty relationship with his intellectual sidekick James Hathaway – and allows him to use his first name at the end of the penultimate series. And he lives on sausage rolls, TV dinners, and chips.

In warmest Sicily, a true and loyal Sicilian, the excitable Commissario Salvo Montalbano, erratically explores brutal murders (he can count the number executed by somebody with brains on the fingers of one hand), against the beautiful but criminal backdrop of small Sicilian towns. He has a volatile and (as yet) unresolved relationship with his equally volatile Livia. He has a confrontational and often violently argumentative relationship with his sidekick Mimì Augello. And he eats his way through endless gastronomic delights, such as *caponata, pasta 'ncasciata* and *melanzane alla parmigiana* provided by his housekeeper Adelina.

Are those England and Italy in a nutshell? *In poche parole*?

What might have happened if some of those fictional worlds collided? Here, perhaps, is the most quintessential collision of them all:

Alice was walking through the wood, wondering what other strange things she might see, when she almost collided with a running figure. She stepped back, and the figure stumbled over her foot, turned a somersault, and crashed into a tree.

'Are you alright?' said Alice, much concerned, but the boy – at least she thought it was a boy – merely got up and dusted himself down.

'I'm alright,' he said. 'It helps being made of wood. You don't feel things,' and he burst into tears.

'But if you don't feel things,' Alice said, 'why are you crying?'

'I don't know,' said the wooden boy. 'Perhaps I'll stop,' and he stopped.

Alice thought that she had not seen a more curious figure all day. He seemed to have been burned around the legs, and bitten around the arms, and his nose and ears seemed to be longer than one might have expected.

Have you seen a fox and a cat?' the boy said. 'They've been chasing me. Is anybody chasing you?'

'No,' Alice said. 'Nobody ever chases me. Why are the fox and the cat chasing you?'

'They want to steal my money,' said the boy, 'and then they'll probably hang me from a tree until I'm dead.'

This didn't seem a very comfortable arrangement to Alice. 'Why don't you just go home?' she asked.

'I really, really want to,' said the boy, bursting into tears again. 'My poor papa is waiting for me, heartbroken. I let him down about buying my school book and I have been a wicked and disobedient boy.'

'In that case,' Alice said (she was becoming rather tired of this conversation) 'you had better go home.'

'Oh no,' said the boy. 'This is MUCH more fun,' and he leaped up and disappeared into the wood. A few seconds later a fox and a cat, carrying wicked looking knives, ran past Alice and disappeared into the wood after the boy.

Alice gazed at the spot where they had vanished, and walked slowly on. 'What a strange thing to worry about,' she thought. 'Why, anybody can just pick up a school book, and I can't imagine anyone waiting for me,' and she walked calmly on into the dark wood.

Alice versus Pinocchio

For Italy may we present a wooden puppet, whose adventures include burning his own feet off, being eaten by a whale, being hung and dying, coming back to life and being turned into a donkey and finally being transformed into a real boy...

And for England – a well-disciplined little girl, who dreams that she falls down a rabbit hole, grows tall and small and meets a lot of eccentric characters, plays a lot of word games, recites strangely distorted poetry ... and wakes up again...

The whole world knows about them: you can hear about the adventures of Pinocchio or 'Pinokyo' in Swahili, or of Alice or Alitiji in Pitjanjatjara – the language of Australian natives around Oluru (or Ayer's Rock). One of the (several) Italian versions of *Alice's Adventures in Wonderland* is sub-titled *Una lucida invenzione, la creazione poetica di una 'lolita' vittoriana* (we should not forget that *Alice* was translated into Russian by one Vladimir Nabokov).

References to Pinocchio and his nose, and the relationship between nose growing and lying, are everywhere, not just in books, but in advertising, jokes, cartoons, and toys. 'Wonderland' – worldwide – is a land of nonsense, usually where everyone but yourself is mad! Both books have become embedded in the self-images of their nations – and not necessarily in a complimentary way. Not long ago, an Italian magazine posed the question: 'Il paese di Pinocchio è davvero più bugiardo di tanti altri?' ('is the country of Pinocchio more of a liar than other countries?'); equally, English journalists cite *Alice* almost every day: 'Only in the Alice in Wonderland world of Brighton's political scene could you find...' The most popular satirical show in Italy is Maurizio Crozza's one-man show, which exposes the nonsense of Italian politics. The politicians that he imitates often say completely surreal things to which his comment is invariably 'Certo. L'Italia è il paese delle meraviglie!' ('Of course – Italy is Wonderland'). Not surprisingly, his show is called *Crozza nel paese delle meraviglie*!

llustration by Enrico Mazzanti from the first edition of *Le avventure di Pinocchio* **(1883)**

Pinocchio is in one sense 'everyperson' – as Benedetto Croce said: *'il legno in cui è intagliato Pinocchio è l'umanità'* ('the wood

Pinocchio is carved from is the human race'): in another sense, he is all Italian. He is passionate, impulsive, unreliable, warm-hearted (and big-hearted), well-intentioned and easily swayed. Suzanne Steward-Steinberg in her book *The Pinocchio Effect, On Making Italians* suggests that Pinocchio is the epitome of *scioltezza* – the Italian looseness or elasticity of mind and body: 'The Italian refuses all civic ties and instead produces personalized relations of power'. He may be wild and thoughtless and ungovernable but he is intensely loyal, especially to family – and he is, finally, unbeatable. The whole book is a kaleidoscope of action and reaction, adventure and return – it is a book of extremes, of energetic invention. Things *happen*. But, above all this apparent chaos, there is Pinocchio's search for his father, his family – a search for humanity.

Illustration by John Tenniel from the first edition of *Alice's Adventures in Wonderland* **(1865)**

Alice could hardly be more different. Her book, like Pinocchio's, is a picaresque, a string of incidents held together by

Alice herself, but Alice's progress is, for all the mad adults that swirl around her, very ordered and linear. Alice – like the Englishman in Noël Coward's classic satire 'Mad Dogs and Englishmen Go Out in the Mid-Day Sun' – has a calm, self-contained, reserved, polite and stoic attitude to life. She is often puzzled, sometimes a little worried, but otherwise her *sang froid* is unblemished. Pinocchio is battered and scarred and singed and chewed (among much else); Alice gets some leaves in her hair, and moves through a world of inferiors (whether they are kings or queens or not), subjecting every rule to cool logic and contemptuously flicking aside eccentric adults. For Alice, the rest of the world is simply deviant. Nor does she care greatly about anyone – for her, adults are nothing more than collections of meaningless rules, which she can overturn at any time (in her dreams).

And so the world knows that Pinocchio means *Italian* and Alice means *English.*

Even the Italians and English know this and seem to be happy with it, which is perhaps surprising, given that neither character is uniformly attractive

The books are, in a sense, frozen in time – they sum up unconscious national attitudes deriving from half-forgotten circumstances. *Pinocchio* is the product of an unstable moment in Italian history: it is a book of the *Risorgimento* ('rising again' or 'resurgence'), a story of a poor and hungry nation – with an intellectual hunger for education. This is a very Italian story written at a time when the political unification of Italy had been (nearly) completed and it was still not clear what it meant for a new nation made of different languages, dialects and customs to have to share common values as citizens. Poverty (*la miseria*) is what characterizes Pinocchio's family life: when Mangiafuoco (the puppeteer Fire-Eater) enquires what his father's trade is, Pinocchio replies: 'that of a poor man' (*fa il povero*). In contrast, Alice's world is one of high Victorian confidence: the Empire was hardly challenged – and if cracks of doubt are beginning to show, that doesn't bother Alice.

Alice is *safe,* even if her world is sleepwalking towards disaster: the eccentrics, the homicidal queen, the demented king-judge, are all ultimately harmless, and anything unsettling in the dream can be brushed away and ignored like the leaves. And even if they aren't, Alice is ready for them. Pinocchio *isn't* safe, and his world is full of surprises – not all of them pleasant – but he's up for anything.

Alice and Pinocchio may not be the perfect images of their parent nations, but if we are looking for the essence of England, and the essence of Italy, then we could do a lot worse than to add *Alice's Adventures in Wonderland* and *Le avventure di Pinocchio* to our traveller's bookshelf.

More reading...

Peter Ackroyd, *Albion. At the Origins of the English Imagination* (London: Vintage Books, 2014)

Pellegrino Artusi [1891] *La scienza in cucina e l'arte di mangiar bene* (Milano: Giunti, 2002)

Clive Aslet, *The English House. The Story of a Nation at Home* (London: Bloomsbury, 2008)

John Ayto, *A Gourmet's Guide. Food and Drink from A to Z* (Oxford: Oxford University Press, 1994)

Mrs Beeton [1861] *Book of Household Management* (Oxford: Oxford University Press, 2000)
– *Book of Household Cookery* (London: Ward Lock, 1950)

Edward C. Banfield, *The Moral Basis of a Backward Society* (New York and London: The Free Press, 1958)

Leonardo Benevolo, *Le città nella storia d'Europa* (Milano: Laterza, 1993)

Roberto Bertinetti, *Dai Beatles a Blair: La cultura inglese contemporanea* (Roma: Carocci, 2001)

Bill Bryson, *Notes From A Small Island* (London: Black Swan, 1996)

Alberto Capatti and Massimo Montanari, *Italian Cuisine. A Cultural History* (New York: Colombia University Press, 2003)

Martin Clark, *Modern Italy 1871-1995* (London and New York: Longman, 1996)

Robin Cohen, *Frontiers of Identity: the British and the Others* (London and New York: Longman, 1994)

Robert Colls, *Identity of England* (New York: Oxford University Press, 2002)

Elizabeth David [1954] *Italian Food* (London: Penguin, 1998)

Peter Davidson, *The Idea of North* (London: Reaktion Books, 2005)

Holger Ehling, *Finding England. An Ausländer's Guide to Perfidious Albion* (London: The Armchair Traveller, 2012)

Antony Easthope, *Englishness and National Culture* (London and New York: Routledge, 1999)

Jean-Louis Frandrin and Massimo Montanari (eds.) *Food. A Culinary History* (New York: Columbia University Press, 1999)

Giovanni Floris, *Separati in patria. Nord contro sud: perché l'Italia è sempre più divisa* (Milano: Rizzoli, 2009)

Kate Fox, *Watching the English. The Hidden Rules of English Behaviour* (London: Hodder and Stoughton, 2004)

Krishan Kumar, *The Making of English National Identity* (Cambridge: Cambridge University Press, 2003)

Ernesto Galli della Loggia, *L'identità italiana* (Bologna: Il Mulino, 2010)

David Gilmour, *The Pursuit of Italy* (London: Penguin, 2012)

Paul Ginsburg, *Storia d'Italia 1943-1996. Famiglia, società, stato* (Torino: Einaudi, 1998)

Henry Hitchings, *Sorry! The English and their Manners* (London: John Murray, 2013)

W.G. Hoskins, *The Making of the English Landscape* (London: Penguin, 1955)

Riccardo Jacona, *Se questi sono gli uomini. Italia 2012. La strage delle donne* (Milano: Chiarelettere, 2012)

Tobias Jones, *The Dark Heart of Italy* (London: Faber & Faber, 2003)

Fiamma Lussana, *Il movimento femminista in Italia. Esperienze, storie, memorie* (Roma: Carocci, 2009)

Sarah Lyall, *A Field Guide to the British* (London: Cuercos, 2008)

Stuart Maconie, *Pies and Prejudice. In Search of the North* (London: Ebury Press, 2008)
– *The People's Songs. The Story of Modern Britain in 50 Songs* (London: Ebury Press, 2013)

Andrew Marr, *The Making of Modern Britain. From Queen Victoria to VE Day* (London: Macmillan, 2009)

Massimo Montanari, *L'identità italiana in cucina* (Milano: Laterza, 2010)
– *Il riposo della polpetta e altre storie intorno al cibo* (Milano: Laterza, 2009)

Donatella Montini, 'Teaching Italian as a Foreign Language: Notes on Linguistic and Pragmatic Strategies in Florio's *Fruits*', *Textus* XXIV (2011)

Harry Mount, *How England Made the English* (London: Penguin, 2013)

Lindsay Myers, *Making the Italians. Poetics and Politics of Italian Children's Fantasy* (Oxford and Bern: Peter Lang, 2012)

Silvana Patriarca, *Italianità. La costruzione del carattere nazionale* (Milano: Laterza, 2010)

Jeremy Paxman, *The English* (London: Penguin, 2007)

Alessandra Petrina, 'Perfit Readiness: Elizabeth learning and using Italian', in Carlo M. Bajetta, Guillaume Coatalen and Jonathan Gibson (eds.) *Elizabeth I's Foreign Correspondence. Letters, Rhetoric, and Politics* (Basingstoke: Palgrave Macmillan, 2014)

Paola Guagliumi, *Guida al contrario per capire gli inglesi* (Viterbo: Stampa Alternativa, 2004)

Beppe Severgnini, *An Italian in Britain* (Milan: Rizzoli, 2003)
– *Inglesi* (Milano: Rizzoli, 2014)
– *La Bella Figura: an Insider's Guide to the Italian Mind* (London: Hodder and Stoughton, 2007)
– *La testa degli italiani* (Milano: Rizzoli, 2008)
– *La pancia degli italiani. Berlusconi spiegato ai posteri* (Milano: Rizzoli, 2011)
– *La vita è un viaggio* (Milano: Rizzoli, 2014)

Nigel Slater, *Eating for England* (London: Fourth Estate, 2007)

Anthony D. Smith, *National Identity* (London: Penguin, 1981)

Paolo Sorcinelli, *Gli italiani e il cibo. Dalla polenta ai crackers* (Milano: Bruno Mondadori, 1999)

Suzanne Stewart-Steinberg, *The Pinocchio Effect. On Making Italians 1860-1920* (Chicago and London: University of Chicago Press, 2007)

Mike Storry and Peter Childs (eds.) *British Cultural Identities* (London: Routledge, 1997)

Carlo Tullio-Altan, *Gli Italiani in Europa. Profilo storico comparato delle identità nazionali europee* (Bologna: Il Mulino, 1999)

Francesco Tuccari, *La nazione* (Milano: Laterza, 2000)

Martin Wainwright, *True North. In Praise of England's Better Half* (London: Guardian Books, 2010)

Thanks to...

- The Italophile and Anglophile friends and colleagues with whom we have shared wine and restaurant tables and conversations about the book, and in particular to students for their many suggestions, some of which were publishable

- Alberto, who ventured into the most private parts of society, where no investigator had gone before

- Beppe Severgnini, who has a knack of pinpointing what many Italians in England and many English in Italy have been thinking and didn't dare put on paper

- Maurizio, the 21st century's answer to Marcello Mastroianni (but taller) for introducing us to Patrician Press

- Francesca and Daniele, who fed us so well at their wedding and whose wedding menu is in the book

- Leonardo da Vinci, Marco Polo, Cristoforo Colombo, and Galileo Galilei for founding airports in convenient parts of Italy[29]

- All the people in England to whom Laura has desperately tried to explain why so many Italians voted for Berlusconi for twenty years (never having voted for him herself)

- And the Austrians for inventing Spritz and then leaving Italy so that the Italians could drink it in peace!

---

[29] Rome, Venice, Genoa, and Pisa